E-banking in India

Challenges and Opportunities

E-banking in India

Challenges and Opportunities

Edited by

R.K. Uppal and Rimpi Jatana

New Century Publications
New Delhi, India

NEW CENTURY PUBLICATIONS
4800/24, Bharat Ram Road,
Ansari Road, Daryaganj,
New Delhi-110 002

Tel.: 23247798, 65396605
Telefax: 011-41017798
E-mail: indiatax@vsnl.com
www.newcenturypublications.com

Editorial office:
34, Gujranwala Town, Part-2,
Delhi - 110 009
Tel.: 27247805, 27464774

First Published 2007

ISBN: 81-7708-137-3

Published by New Century Publications and printed at Singhal Print Media, New Delhi -110 005

PRINTED IN INDIA

The Book

Finland was the first country in the world to have taken a lead in E-banking. In India, it was ICICI Bank which initiated E-banking as early as 1997 under the brand name *Infinity*.

Electronic banking (E-banking) is a generic term encompassing internet banking, telephone banking, mobile banking etc. In other words, it is a process of delivery of banking services and products through electronic channels such as telephone, internet, cell phone etc. The concept and scope of E-banking is still evolving.

E-banking facilitates an effective payment and accounting system thereby enhancing the speed of delivery of banking services considerably. While E-banking has improved efficiency and convenience, it has also posed several challenges to the regulators and supervisors.

Several initiatives taken by the Government of India as well as the Reserve Bank of India (RBI) have facilitated the development of E-banking in India. The Government of India enacted the IT Act, 2000 with effect from October 17, 2000, which provides legal recognition to electronic transactions and other means of electronic commerce.

The RBI has been gearing up to upgrading itself as a regulator and supervisor of the technologically dominated financial system. It issued guidelines on *risks and control in computer and telecommunication system* in February 1998 to all the banks advising them to evaluate the risks inherent in the systems and put in place adequate control mechanisms to address these risks, which can be broadly put under three heads, *viz.* IT environment risks, IT operations risks and product risks.

The existing regulatory framework over banks has also been extended to E-banking. It covers various issues that fall within the framework of technology, security standards and legal and regulatory issues.

This book contains 12 articles by scholars specialising in the area of banking. It will be useful for all those who want to understand recent technological developments in Indian banking.

Editors' Profile

Dr. R.K. Uppal did his M.A. in economics from Punjabi University, Patiala in 1986. Thereafter, he obtained M.Phil. degree from MDU, Rohtak in 1987 and Ph.D. degree from Punjabi University, Patiala in 2003. Specialising in banking and finance, Dr. Uppal has six books to his credit and has published a number of papers on the subject in reputed journals and presented papers in national and international conferences. Presently, he is head of the Department of Economics, DAV College, Malout, Punjab and Principal Investigator of a UGC-financed research project on Indian banking.

Mrs. Rimpi Jatana (M.Com., PGDCA) is presently a research scholar in Punjab School of Management Studies, Punjabi University, Patiala and a Project Fellow in a UGC-financed research project, D.A.V. College, Malout, Punjab. Her areas of specialisation is banking and finance in which she has published more than 13 research papers and articles in different journals.

Editors' Note on the Book

Electronic banking (E-banking) is a generic term encompassing internet banking, telephone banking, mobile banking etc. In other words, it is a process of delivery of banking services and products through electronic channels such as telephone, internet, cell phone etc. The concept and scope of E-banking is still evolving.

E-banking facilitates an effective payment and accounting system thereby enhancing the speed of delivery of banking services considerably. While the E-banking has improved efficiency and convenience, it has also posed several challenges to the regulators and supervisors.

Several initiatives taken by the Government of India as well as the Reserve Bank of India (RBI) have facilitated the development of E-banking in India. As a regulator and supervisor, the RBI has made considerable progress in consolidating the existing payment and settlement systems, and in upgrading technology with a view to establishing an efficient, integrated and secure system functioning in a real-time environment, which has further helped the development of E-banking in India. The Government of India enacted the IT Act, 2000 with effect from October 17, 2000, which provides legal recognition to electronic transactions and other means of electronic commerce.

Finland was the first country in the world to have taken a lead in E-banking. Up to one-third of bank customers in Finland and Sweden take advantage of E-banking. In India, it was ICICI Bank which initiated E-banking as early as 1997 under the brand name *Infinity*.

Like many other countries, India does not have specific regulatory laws for E-banking. The existing regulatory framework over banks has been extended to E-banking as well. However, certain guidelines have been issued to banks to recognise the risks arising from electronic modes and to devise control mechanisms that are needed to mitigate such risks. Banks offering E-banking services in India are required to comply with these guidelines.

The RBI has been gearing up to upgrading itself as a regulator and supervisor of the technologically dominated financial system. It issued guidelines on *risks and control in computer and telecommunication system* in February 1998 to all the banks advising them to evaluate the risks inherent in the systems and put in place adequate control mechanisms to address these risks, which can be broadly put under three heads, *viz.* IT environment risks, IT operations risks and product risks.

The existing regulatory framework over banks has also been extended to E-banking. It covers various issues that fall within the framework of technology, security standards and legal and regulatory issues. Virtual banks, which have no offices and function only on-line are not permitted to offer E-banking services in India and that only banks licensed under the Banking Regulation Act, 1949 and having a physical presence in India are allowed to offer such services. Further, banks are required to report to the RBI every breach or failure of security systems and procedures in E-banking, while the RBI at its discretion may decide to commission special audit/inspection of such banks.

As per recent guidelines, banks no longer need any prior approval of the RBI for offering E-banking services. Nevertheless, banks must have their internet policy and they need to ensure that it is in line with parameters as set by the Working Group on Internet Banking in India (Chairman: S.R. Mittal) 2001.

Reviewing the technological developments in Indian commercial banks, the *Economic Survey*, 2006-07 observed, "The banking sector in India is adapting itself to rapid innovations in technology particularly on the information-based technology front to impart efficiency in providing wide range of products and services to the public at large. Computerisation of banking operations had received high importance in 2005-06. Since September 1999 to March 2006, PSBs incurred an expenditure of Rs. 10,676 crore on computerisation and development of communication networks. Out of 27 PSBs, branches of as many as 10 PSBs were 100 per cent computerised, while more than 50 per cent branches of 12 banks were computerised by end-March 2006.

The number of branches providing 'core banking solutions' (CBS) in recent years is increasing rapidly. Under CBS, a number of services are being provided such as 'anywhere banking', 'everywhere access', and quick transfer of funds in an efficient manner and at reasonable cost. New private sector banks, foreign banks and a few old private sector banks have already put in place CBS; PSBs are increasingly adopting a similar system. The total number of branches of PSBs offering CBS increased from 11.0 per cent as on March 31, 2005. to 28.9 per cent as on March 31, 2006.

Total number of Automated Teller Machines (ATMs) installed by the banks were 21,147 at end-March 2006. Nationalised banks with 7,165 ATMs were the largest providers of the ATM service followed by new private banks (6,112), SBI group (5,443), old private banks (1,547) and foreign banks (880).

This book contains 12 articles by scholars specialising in the area of banking. Thanks are due to all of them for their contributions and co-operation. Thanks are also due to the editors of New Century Publications, New Delhi for improving and standardising the texts of papers included in this volume.

June 2007

R.K. Uppal
Rimpi Jatana

List of Contributors

R.K. Uppal	Head, Department of Economics, D.A.V. College, Malout (Punjab).
S. Ganesan	Director, KCT School of Business, Coimbatore.
S. Shanmuga Pria	Faculty in Finance, DJ Academy for Managerial Excellence, Coimbatore.
Puja Arora	Lecturer in Commerce, SCD Government College for Boys, Ludhiana.
Deepak Kumar	Lecturer in Commerce, Kamla Lohtia S.D. College, Ludhiana.
Monika Kansal	Senior Lecturer in Commerce, Kamla Lohtia S.D. College, Ludhiana.
Seema Kapoor	Lecturer, Department of Economics, K.C.W., Ludhiana.
Deepak Dhingra	Lecturer, Department of Commerce, KLSD College, Ludhiana.
Preety Sharma	Lecturer, Department of Commerce, R.S.D. College, Ferozepur.
Pooja Mehta	Lecturer, Department of Commerce, R.S.D. College, Ferozepur.
Neetu Gupta	Lecturer, Department of Economics, Khalsa College for Women, Ludhiana.
Shashi Kapoor	Lecturer in Commerce, Gobindgarh Public College, Alour.
Neelam Khullar	Lecturer in Commerce, Kamla Lohtia S.D. College, Ludhiana.
Leena Kakkar	Lecturer, Department of Commerce, Dev Samaj College for Women, Ferozepur City.
Rimpi Jatana	Project Fellow, UGC-MRP, DAV College, Malout.
Nittu Gupta	DAV College, Malout (Punjab).
Shiwani Gupta	Lecturer, Department of Commerce, KMV College, Jalandhar.
Neetu Khanna	Lecturer, Department of Commerce, KMV College, Jalandhar.
Nitu Gupta	Lecturer, Department of Commerce, Khalsa College for Women, Ludhiana.

Contents

1

Banking Sector Reforms and E-banking in India

R.K. Uppal

1.1 Post-Independence Developments in Banking Sector

1.1.1 Pre-nationalisation Period: The year 1969 was a landmark in the history of commercial banking in India. In July of that year, the government nationalised 14 major commercial banks of the country. In April 1980, government nationalised 6 more commercial banks.

In 1951, when the First Five Year Plan (1951-56) was launched, the development of rural India was accorded the highest priority. The All India Rural Credit Survey Committee recommended the creation of a State-partnered and State-sponsored bank by taking over the Imperial Bank of India and integrating with it, the former State-owned or State-associated banks. Accordingly, an Act was passed in the Parliament in May 1955 and the State Bank of India was constituted on July 1, 1955. Later, the State Bank of India (Subsidiary Banks) Act was passed in 1959 enabling the State Bank of India to take over eight former State-associated banks as its subsidiaries.

During the pre-nationalisation period, the industrial sector claimed the lion's share in bank credit. Within the industry, the large-scale sector cornered the bulk of credit and the share of small-scale industries was marginal. There were many reasons for the dominance of large industrial companies in the banking sector. Firstly, many commercial banks were under the ownership/control of big industrial houses. Secondly, through common directors (called interlocking of directorship), many commercial banks were connected with industrial and business houses, facilitating the flow of credit to large industries. Thirdly, the established industrial houses could obtain industrial licenses easily and on that basis, appropriate long- term bank credit.

A disturbing feature of the pre-nationalisation banking policy was the negligible share of agricultural sector in bank credit. This share hovered around 2 per cent of total commercial bank credit. The privately-owned commercial banks were neither interested nor geared to meet the risky and small credit requirements of the farmers. Similarly, the share of other non-industrial sectors in bank credit was also low.

Since the commercial banks were under the control of big industrialists, the lendable funds of the banks were sometimes used to finance socially undesirable activities like hoarding of essential commodities.

1.1.2 Post-nationalisation Period: As already noted, leading commercial banks of the country were nationalised in 1969 with the following objectives in view:

- To break the ownership and control of banks by a few business families.
- To prevent concentration of wealth and economic power.
- To mobilise savings of the masses from every nook and corner of the country.
- To pay greater attention to the credit needs of the priority sectors like agriculture and small industries.

The post-nationalisation period witnessed a remarkable expansion in the banking and financial system. The biggest achievement of nationalisation was the reallocation of sectoral credit in favour of agriculture, small industries and exports which formed the core of the priority sector. Within agriculture, credit for the procurement of food grains (food credit) was a major item. Other agricultural activities preferred for credit included poultry farming, dairy, and piggeries. Certain other sectors of the economy which also received attention for credit allocation were: professionals and self-employed persons, artisans and weaker sections of society. Conversely, there was a sharp fall in bank credit to large-scale industries. However, the share of small-scale industry registered an upward trend.

Nationalisation of commercial banks was a mixed blessing. After nationalisation there was a shift of emphasis from industry to agriculture. The country witnessed rapid expansion in bank branches, even in rural areas. Branch expansion programme led to mobilisation of savings from all parts of the country. Nationalised banks were able to pay attention to the credit needs of weaker sections, artisans and self-employed. However, bank nationalisation created its own problems like excessive bureaucratisation, red-tapism and disruptive tactics of trade unions of bank employees.

1.2 Banking Sector Reforms since 1991

Until the early 1990s, the banking sector suffered from lack of competition, low capital base, low productivity and high intermediation cost. Commenting on the performance of the nationalised banks, the Reserve Bank of India observed, "After the nationalisation of large banks in 1969 and 1980, the Government-owned banks have dominated the banking sector. The role of technology was minimal and the quality of service was not given adequate importance. Banks also did not follow proper risk management systems and the prudential standards were weak. All these resulted in poor asset quality and low profitability." [1]

Prior to reforms, the Indian Government determined the quantum, allocation and the price of credit, a situation referred to as *financial repression* by some experts.

It was in this backdrop, that wide-ranging banking sector reforms in India were introduced as an integral part of the economic reforms initiated in the early 1990s. Reforms in the commercial banking sector had two distinct phases.

1.2.1 The First Phase: The first phase of reforms implemented subsequent to the release of the Report of the Committee on Financial System (Chairman: M. Narasimham), 1992 (or Narasimham Committee I) focussed mainly on enabling and strengthening measures. The Committee was guided by the fundamental assumption that the resources of the banks come from the general public and held by the banks in trust. These resources have to be deployed for maximum benefit of their owners, i.e. the depositors. This assumption automatically implies that even the Government has no business to endanger the solvency, health and efficiency of the nationalised banks. According to the Committee, the poor financial shape and low efficiency of public sector banks was due to: (a) extensive degree of central direction of their operations, particularly in terms of investment, credit allocation and branch expansion and (b) excessive political interference, resulting into failure of commercial banks to operate on the basis of their commercial judgement and in the framework of internal economy. Despite opposition from trade unions and some political parties, the Government accepted all the major recommendations of the Committee some of which have already been implemented.

1.2.2 The Second Phase: The second phase of reforms, implemented subsequent to the recommendations of the Committee on Banking Sector Reforms (Chairman: M. Narasimham), 1998 (or Narasimham Committee II) placed greater emphasis on structural measures and improvement in standards of disclosure and levels of transparency in order to align the Indian standards with international best practices.

1.2.3 Objectives of Banking Sector Reforms: The key objective of reforms in the banking sector in India has been to enhance the stability and efficiency of banks. To achieve this objective, various reform measures were initiated that could be categorised broadly into three main groups:

- enabling measures,
- strengthening measures and
- institutional measures.

Enabling measures were designed to create an environment where banks could respond optimally to market signals on the basis of commercial considerations. Salient among these included reduction in statutory pre-emptions so as to release greater funds for commercial lending, interest rate deregulation to enable price discovery, granting of operational autonomy to banks and liberalisation of the entry norms for financial intermediaries.

The strengthening measures aimed at reducing the vulnerability of banks in the face of fluctuations in the economic environment. These included, inter alia, capital adequacy, income recognition, asset classification and provisioning norms, exposure norms, improved levels of transparency, and disclosure standards.

Institutional framework conducive to development of banks needs to be developed. Salient among these include reforms in the legal framework pertaining to banks and creation of new institutions.

1.2.4 Contents of Banking Sector Reforms: Banking sector reforms since 1991 have included, among others, the following:

- granting operational autonomy to banks,
- liberalisation of entry norms for banks,
- reduction in statutory pre-emptions so as to release greater funds for commercial lending,
- deregulation of interest rates,
- relaxation in investment norms for banks,
- easing of restrictions in respect of banks' foreign currency investments and
- withdrawal of reserve requirements on inter-bank borrowings.

Thus, financial repression has eased substantially with the deregulation of interest rates and substantial removal of credit allocation.

A. Cash Reserve Ratio (CRR): Scheduled banks in India are required statutorily to hold cash reserves, called cash reserve ratio (CRR), with the RBI. Increase/decrease in CRR is used by the RBI as an instrument of monetary control, particularly to mop up excess increases in the supply of money. This power was given to RBI in 1956.

Narasimham Committee I recommended that RBI should rely on open market operations increasingly and reduce its dependence on CRR. This would reduce the amount of cash balances of the banks with the RBI enabling them to increase their revenues through more investments. It proposed that CRR should be progressively reduced from the then existing level of 15 per cent to 3 to 5 per cent.

CRR was gradually lowered from its peak at 15 per cent during July 1989 to April 1993 to 8.0 per cent in April 2000. It stood at 5 per cent effective October 2, 2004. In this connection, the Ninth Five Year Plan (1997-2002) remarked, "the level of the cash reserve ratio (CRR) that is to be maintained by the Indian banks is considerably higher than the international levels which are specified for prudential reasons. Although in recent years there has been significant reduction in the CRR from 15 per cent to 10 per cent and also the interest paid on CRR deposits with the RBI has been raised from 3.5 per cent to 4.5 per cent, there is a view that the CRR should be reduced even further, preferably to 3 per cent." [2]

B. Statutory Liquidity Ratio (SLR): Apart from the CRR, banks in India are also subject to statutory liquidity requirement. Under this requirement, commercial banks along with other financial institutions like Life Insurance Corporation of India (LIC), the General Insurance Corporation (GIC) and the Provident Funds are required under law to invest prescribed minimum proportions of their total assets/liabilities in government securities and other approved securities. The underlying philosophy of this provision is to allocate total bank credit between the government and the rest of the economy. The assurance of a certain minimum share of bank credit to the government affects the borrowings of the government from the RBI and hence serves as a tool of quantitative monetary control.

The SLR provision has created a captive market for government securities which increases automatically with the growth in the liabilities of the banks. Moreover, it has kept the cost of the debt to the government low in view of the generally low rate of interest on government securities.

Narasimham Committee I asked the Government to reduce the SLR from the then existing 38.5 per cent to 25 per cent over a period of five years. A reduction in the SLR levels would leave more funds with the banks which could allocate them to promote agriculture, industry and trade. The Committee further recommended that Government borrowing rates should be progressively market-related so that higher rates would help banks to increase their income from their SLR investments.

SLR was reduced from its peak of 38.5 per cent during September 1990 to 25 per cent in October 1997.

C. Structure of Interest Rates: Narasimham Committee I recommended that the level and structure of interest rates in the country should be broadly determined by market forces. All controls and regulations on interest rates on lending should be removed.

The country has moved towards liberalised credit allocation mechanism and reduced direct control over interest rates by the monetary authorities. Interest rate slabs have been gradually reduced from 20 to 3. Similarly, interest rates have been deregulated on the high slabs of bank rates. The purpose of deregulation is to promote healthy competition among the banks and encourage their operational efficiency. Scheduled banks have now the freedom to set interest rates on their deposits subject to minimum floor rate (4.5 per cent) and maximum ceiling rate (11 per cent).

Prime lending rates of banks for commercial credit are now entirely within the purview of the banks and are not set by the RBI. The domestic interest rates which are still subject to regulation are the rate of interest on saving accounts and rates of interest on export credit. In line with the decline in inflation rate and also in view of the importance of lower real interest rates in accelerating industrial growth and boosting India's competitiveness abroad, RBI reduced the Bank Rate [3] from 8 per cent to 7 per cent, effective April 2, 2000. Rate of interest on saving deposits of commercial banks was also reduced from 4.5 per cent to 4.0 per cent. Following these measures, the structure of interest rates in India has come closer to ruling international rates.

D. Organisation of Banking Structure: Narasimham Committee I proposed a substantial reduction in the number of public sector banks through mergers and acquisitions. The broad pattern should consist of:

- 3 or 4 large banks which could become international in character.
- 8 or 10 national banks with a network of branches throughout the country.
- local banks whose operations would be generally confined to a specific region.
- rural banks whose operations will be confined to rural areas.

Significantly, Narasimham Committee I recommended that RBI should permit the setting up of new banks in the private sector. It wanted a positive declaration from the Government that there would be no more nationalisation of banks. It further recommended that there should not be any difference in treatment between the public sector banks and the private sector banks.

It recommended that RBI should follow a more liberal policy in respect of allowing the foreign banks to open branches in India and they should be subjected to the same requirements as are applicable to the Indian banks.

In January 1993, RBI had issued guidelines for licensing of new banks in the private sector. It had granted licenses to 10 banks which are presently in business. Based on a review of experience gained on the functioning of new private sector banks, revised guidelines were issued in January 2000. Following are the major revised provisions:

- Initial minimum paid-up capital shall be Rs. 200 crore which will be raised to Rs. 300 crore within three years of commencement of business.
- Contribution of promoters shall be a minimum of 40 per cent of the paid-up capital of the bank at any point of time. This contribution of 40 per cent shall be locked in for five years from the date of licensing of the bank.
- While augmenting capital to Rs. 300 crore within three years, promoters shall bring in at least 40 per cent of the fresh capital which will also be locked in for five years.
- NRI participation in the primary equity of a new bank shall be to the maximum extent of 40 per cent.

E. Duality of Control: Narasimham Committee I recommended removal of duality of control over the banking system by the banking department of the Finance Ministry on the one hand, and by the RBI on the other hand. The Committee desired the RBI to assume full responsibility of overseeing the functioning of the banking system.

F. Abolition of Selective Credit Controls (SCCs): SCCs, introduced in India in 1956, pertain to regulation of credit for specific purposes. The techniques of SCCs used by the RBI include fixing minimum margins for lending against securities, ceiling on maximum advances to individual borrowers against stocks of certain commodities, and minimum discriminatory rates of interest prescribed for certain kinds of advances. SCCs have been used mainly to prevent the speculative holding of essential commodities like foodgrains to prevent price rise.

Selective credit controls have been abolished in the post-liberalisation period.

G. Other Measures: Credit restrictions for purchase of consumer durables have been removed/relaxed. Similarly, coverage of priority sector has been enlarged by the inclusion of software, agro-processing industries and venture capital. These measures have given the banks the much-needed flexibility to manage their asset portfolios.

Commenting on the success of banking sector reforms, the Reserve Bank of India observed, "There is evidence to suggest that competition in the banking industry has intensified. Significant improvement was also discernible in the various parameters of efficiency, especially intermediation costs, which declined significantly. Profitability of commercial banks, on the whole, improved significantly despite a decline in spread and higher provisioning following the introduction and subsequent tightening of prudential norms." [4]

1.3 Current Issues in Indian Banking

Despite substantial improvements in the banking sector, some issues have to be addressed over time as the reform process is entrenched further. The discussion on banking developments revolves around on a wide range of issues like:

- overall redrawing of boundaries between the State ownership of financial entities and private sector ones.
- public sector character of the banking sector and efficiency.
- dilution of the government stake and its impact on the performance of the banking sector.
- corporate governance in banks and other segments of the financial system.
- transparency of policies and practices of monetary and financial agencies and accountability.
- prudential requirements of market participants together with comprehensive and efficient oversight of the financial system.
- maintenance of best practices in accounting and auditing, as also collection, processing and dissemination of symmetric and detailed information to meet the market needs.
- Relevance of Development Finance Institutions (DFIs).

The commonality among these concerns has given rise to a wide recognition and acceptance of having a set of international standards and best practices that every systemically important country should strive to foster and implement. Financial sector reforms, introduced in the early 1990s in a gradual and sequenced manner, were directed at the removal of various deficiencies from which the system was suffering. The basic objectives of reforms were to make the system more stable and efficient so that it could contribute in accelerating the growth process.

In response to reforms, the Indian banking sector has undergone radical transformation during the 1990s. Reforms have altered the organizational structure, ownership pattern and domain of operations of institutions and infused competition in the financial sector. The competition has forced the institutions to reposition themselves in order to survive and grow. The extensive progress in technology has enabled markets to graduate from outdated systems to modern market design, thus, bringing about a significant reduction in the speed of execution of trades and transaction costs.

With the increasing integration of various segments of financial markets, the distinctions between banks and other financial intermediaries are also getting increasingly blurred. Another important aspect of reforms in the financial sector has been the increased participation of financial institutions, especially banks, in the capital market. These factors have led to increased inter-linkages across financial institutions and markets. While increased inter-linkages are expected to lead to increased efficiency in the resource allocation process and the effectiveness of monetary policy, they also increase the risk of contagion from one segment to another with implications for overall financial stability. This would call for appropriate policy responses during times of crisis. Increased inter-linkages also raise the issue of appropriate supervisory framework.

Banking sector reforms in India are grounded in the belief that competitive efficiency in the real sectors of the economy will not realise its full potential unless the banking sector was reformed as well. Thus, the principal objective of banking sector reforms was to improve the allocative efficiency of resources and accelerate the growth process of the real sector by removing structural deficiencies affecting the performance of banks.

In India, while the banking system continues to play a predominant role, it is significant to note that, as a result of various reform measures, the relative significance of financial markets has increased. This augurs well for the overall stability of the financial system. The East Asian crisis has also underlined the need for a balanced financial system wherein financial markets also play an important role in providing necessary liquidity, especially during times of crisis. Banking system also requires liquidity in times of stress, which only deep and liquid financial markets can provide.

1.4 Future of India's Banking Sector

Banking sector reforms in India are by no means complete. Plans are afoot to modernise the financial system to make it compatible with best international practices.

1.4.1 Vision Document for Payment Systems: 2005-08: In the recent period, the RBI has taken a number of initiatives to strengthen the institutional, technological and procedural framework for the payment and settlement systems. To carry forward these initiatives in an integrated and cohesive manner, a Vision Document for 2005-08 has been prepared after taking into consideration the feedback from the various stakeholders such as banks, technology solution providers, members of public and other experts in the field. The Vision Document sets out the roadmap for implementing the vision for payment and settlement systems within the next three years. The key themes of the action plans identified in the Vision Document are safety, security, soundness and efficiency (Triple-S and E). While safety in payment and settlement systems relates to risk reduction measures, security implies confidence in the integrity of the payment systems. All payment systems are envisaged to be on a sound footing with adequate legal backing for operational procedures and transparency norms. Efficiency enhancements are envisaged by leveraging the benefits of technology for cost effective solutions.

The main action points for payment and settlement systems, 2005-08 as set out in the Vision Document are indicated below:

A. Action Points during 2005-06

- pursuing with Indian Banks' Association and major banks for setting up of a national level entity which will operate all retail payment systems in the country;
- operationalising National Settlement System for all clearings at four metro centres by December 2005;
- finalising the proposed Electronic Funds Transfer (EFT) regulations;
- implementing Stage-2 of RTGS System, *i.e.,* Integrated Accounting System (IAS)-RTGS rollout during which all inter-bank transactions at all major centres would be settled on RTGS platform and paper-based inter-bank clearing will be closed;

- pursuing with RTGS participants to cover all their networked branches under RTGS framework paving way for RTGS-based customer related transactions at about ten thousand branches in the country;
- implementing image-based Cheque Truncation System (CTS) at the National Capital Region (NCR) on a pilot basis;
- preparing minimum standard of operational efficiency at MICR Cheque Processing Centre (CPC);
- making available EFT facility at 500 capital market intensive centres as identified by BSE and NSE;
- setting up Customer Facilitation Centre (CFC) at the RBI for various segments of national payment systems;
- public disclosure from each payment service provider of its standards, terms and conditions under which the payment will be effected and also compensation policy and procedure for any deficiency in services including the setting up of CFC;
- drafting the Red Book on Payment Systems in India; and
- drafting a comprehensive legislation on payment system.

B. Action Points during 2006-07

It is envisaged to:

- complete the tasks initiated during 2005-06;
- extend MICR clearing to 20 additional identified centres;
- ensure that every cheque issued follows MICR format and standards;
- implement EFT systems at a national level through the new retail payment institution;
- make all payment systems in India compliant with the Core Principles for Systemically Important Payment Systems (SIPS);
- increase the reach of payment services by means of tie-up and collaboration with other large coverage entities such as the post offices; and
- facilitate government payments and receipts through electronic mode.

Action Points during 2007-08

- creating off-city back-up arrangements for large value national payment systems such as RTGS and G-Sec Clearing;
- making fully functional the new organisation for retail payment systems with all such payment under its umbrella;
- regulating various payment systems;
- ensuring cheque truncation based clearing at Mumbai, Chennai and Kolkata; and
- covering National Settlement System at all major clearing houses/ clearing organisations in the country.

1.4.2 Financial Sector Technology Vision Document: The RBI released the draft Financial Sector Technology Vision document on May 6, 2005. It provides a broad overview of the thrust areas of the direction provided by the RBI in respect of IT for the financial sector for more than two decades and sets out a roadmap for 2005-08. The Vision document focuses on

- IT for regulation and supervision,
- IT for the Financial Sector and
- IT for Government related functions.

The Vision Document envisages emerging challenges in the form of implementation of standardisation across a variety of hybrid systems at different financial entities, need for decision support systems and the technology to facilitate risk based off-site supervision. It envisions common inter- operable web -based structures for transmission of data relating to regulatory functions and the use of a single centralised database for all information, apart from hiving off the operation of non- critical functions by the RBI. The Vision Document also visualises Institute for Development and Research in Banking Technology (IDRBT) which is to be a premier research institute, concentrating on research and development for the banking and financial sector, providing educational/training facilities and hiving off business related activities.

Recognising the requirements of IT for the financial sector, the Vision Document elucidates the thrust areas of the RBI by providing generic information on various standards and approaches, IS Audit and requisite focus on business continuity plans. The Vision Document proposes that specific attention would be devoted to percolation of technology efforts to all types of banks and all sections of the customers in the banks with specific reference to the rural areas and the use of affordable technology products which can be easily used by the target clientele with inter-shareable resources.

The document also details the use of IT in the Government sector transactions (which has the largest potential to grow significantly in the years to come), with specific attention on the need for business process re-engineering, changes in rules and procedures for aligning them with e-governance in a manner so as to achieve implementable objectives.

1.4.3 Road Map for Foreign Banks in India: At present, foreign banks may operate in India through only one of the three channels, *viz.*

- branches;
- a wholly owned subsidiary (WOS); or
- a subsidiary with an aggregate foreign investment up to a maximum of 74 per cent in a private bank.

With a view to delineate the direction and pace of reform process in this area and to operationalise the extant guidelines of March 4, 2004 in a phased manner, the RBI, on February 28, 2005, released the road map for presence of foreign banks in India. The roadmap is divided into two phases.

A. First Phase: March 2005 to March 2009: During the first phase, between March 2005 and March 2009, foreign banks wishing to establish presence in India for the first time could either choose to operate through branches or set up a 100 per cent WOS, following the one-mode presence criterion. For new and existing foreign banks, it is proposed to go beyond the existing WTO commitment of 12 branches in a year. Foreign banks already operating in India would be permitted to establish presence by way of setting up a WOS or conversion of the existing branches into a WOS. For this purpose, criteria such as ownership pattern, financial soundness, supervisory rating and the international ranking would be considered. The WOS should have a minimum capital of Rs. 300 crore and would need to ensure sound corporate governance. The WOS will be treated on par with the existing branches of foreign banks for branch expansion with flexibility to go beyond the existing WTO commitments and preference for branch expansion in under-banked areas. The RBI may also prescribe market access and national treatment limitation consistent with WTO as also other appropriate limitations to the operations of WOS, consistent with international practices and the country's requirements.

During this phase, permission for acquisition of shareholding in Indian private sector banks by eligible foreign banks will be limited to banks identified by the RBI for restructuring. The RBI may, if it is satisfied that such investment by the foreign bank concerned will be in the long-term interest of all the stakeholders in the investee bank, permit such acquisition. Where such acquisition is by a foreign bank having presence in India, a maximum period of six months would be given for conforming to the 'one form of presence' concept.

B. Second Phase: April 2009 onward: The second phase will commence in April 2009 after a review of the experience gained and after due consultation with all the stakeholders in the banking sector. In this phase, three interconnected issues would be taken up.

First, the removal of limitations on the operations of the WOS and treating them on par with domestic banks to the extent appropriate would be designed and implemented.

Second, the WOS of foreign banks, on completion of a minimum prescribed period of operation, may be allowed to list and dilute their stake so that, consistent with March 5, 2004 guidelines, at least 26 per cent of the paid-up capital of the subsidiary is held by resident Indians at all times. The dilution may be either by way of initial public offer or as an offer for sale.

Third, during this phase, foreign banks may be permitted to enter into merger and acquisition transactions with any private sector bank in India subject to the overall investment limit of 74 per cent.

1.5 What is E-banking?

Electronic banking (E-banking) is a generic term encompassing internet banking, telephone banking, mobile banking etc. In other words, it is a process of delivery of banking services and products through electronic channels such as telephone, internet, cell phone etc. The concept and scope of E-banking is still evolving.

Several initiatives taken by the Government of India as well as the Reserve Bank of India (RBI) have facilitated the development of E-banking in India. As a regulator and supervisor, the RBI has made considerable progress in consolidating the existing payment and settlement systems, and in upgrading technology with a view to establishing an efficient, integrated and secure system functioning in a real-time environment, which has further helped the development of E-banking in India. The Government of India enacted the IT Act, 2000 with effect from October 17, 2000, which provides legal recognition to electronic transactions and other means of electronic commerce.

1.6 E-banking: Global Experiences

Finland was the first country in the world to have taken a lead in E-banking. The Scandinavian countries have the largest number of Internet users, with up to one-third of bank customers in Finland and Sweden taking advantage of E-banking. Internet banking is also widespread in Austria, Korea, Singapore, Spain, Switzerland, *etc*. E-banking facilitates an effective payment and accounting system thereby enhancing the speed of delivery of banking services considerably. While the E-banking has improved efficiency and convenience, it has also posed several challenges to the regulators and supervisors.

In response to the challenges thrown by the Internet banking, regulators and supervisors from various countries have prepared their own mechanism of regulation. There is a matrix of legislation and regulations within the United States that specifically codifies the use of and rights associated with the internet and e-commerce, in general, and electronic banking and internet banking activities, in particular. The concerns of the Federal Reserve are limited to ensuring that Internet banking and other electronic banking services are implemented with proper attention to security, safety and soundness of the bank, and the protection of the banks' customers.

In the UK, there is no specific legislation for regulating E-banking activities. The FSA is neutral on regulations of electronic banking. In Sweden, no formal guidance has been given to examiners by the Sveriges Bank on E-banking. General guidelines apply equally to Internet banking activities. The role of the Bank of Finland has been, as part of general oversight of financial markets in Finland, mainly to monitor the ongoing development of Internet banking without active participation. The Reserve Bank of New Zealand applies the same approach to the regulation of both Internet banking activities and traditional banking activities. There are however, banking regulations that apply only to Internet banking. Supervision is based on public disclosure of information rather than application of detailed prudential rules.

The Monetary Authority of Singapore (MAS) subjects Internet banking to the same prudential standards as traditional banking. The MAS drafted an 'Internet Banking Technology Risk Management Guidelines' in September 2002, which calls upon all banks providing internet banking to establish a sound and robust risk management process. The Hong Kong regulatory approach towards E-banking is less specific in nature. The Hong Kong Monetary Authority (HKMA) expects their banks to undertake a rigorous analysis of the security aspects of their system by getting it reviewed by qualified independent experts.

Like many of these countries, India does not have specific regulatory laws for E-banking. The existing regulatory framework over banks has been extended to Internet banking as well. However, certain guidelines have been issued to banks to recognise the risks arising from electronic modes and to devise control mechanisms that are needed to mitigate such risks. Banks offering the E-banking services in India comply with these guidelines.

1.7 E-banking and RBI

The RBI has been gearing up to upgrading itself as a regulator and supervisor of the technologically dominated financial system. In 1998, it availed the technical assistance project of Department for International Development (DFID), UK for upgrading its supervisory system and adaptation of its supervisory functions to the computerised environment. It issued guidelines on 'risks and control in computer and telecommunication system' in February 1998 to all the banks advising them to evaluate the risks inherent in the systems and put in place adequate control mechanisms to address these risks, which can be broadly put under three heads, *viz.*, IT environment risks, IT operations risks and product risks.

The existing regulatory framework over banks has also been extended to internet banking. These guidelines cover various issues that would fall within the framework of technology, security standards and legal and regulatory issues. Virtual banks, which have no offices and function only on line are not permitted to offer E-banking services in India and that only banks licensed under the Banking Regulation Act and having a physical presence in India are allowed to offer such services. Further, banks are required to report to the RBI every breach or failure of security systems and procedures in Internet banking, while the RBI at its discretion may decide to commission special audit/inspection of such banks. As per recent guidelines, banks no longer need any prior approval of the Reserve Bank for offering the internet banking services. Nevertheless, banks must have their internet policy and they need to ensure that it is in line with parameters as set by the Working Group on Internet Banking in India (2001). Main recommendations of the Working Group are set forth below.

1.8 Main Recommendations of the Working Group on Internet Banking (Chairman: S.R. Mittal), 2001

Reserve Bank of India constituted a Working Group to

examine different issues relating to internet banking and recommend technology, security, legal standards and operational standards keeping in view the international best practices. The Group was headed by the Chief General Manager–in–Charge of the Department of Information Technology and comprised experts from the fields of banking regulation and supervision, commercial banking, law and technology. The Bank also constituted an Operational Group under its Executive Director comprising officers from different disciplines in the bank, who would guide implementation of the recommendations.

The Working Group, as its terms of reference, was to examine different aspects of Internet banking from regulatory and supervisory perspective and recommend appropriate standards for adoption in India, particularly with reference to the following:

1. Risks to the organization and banking system, associated with Internet banking and methods of adopting International best practices for managing such risks.
2. Identifying gaps in supervisory and legal framework with reference to the existing banking and financial regulations, IT regulations, tax laws, depositor protection, consumer protection, criminal laws, money laundering and other cross border issues and suggesting improvements in them.
3. Identifying international best practices on operational and internal control issues, and suggesting suitable ways for adopting the same in India.
4. Recommending minimum technology and security standards, in conformity with international standards and addressing issues like system vulnerability, digital signature ,information system audit etc.
5. Clearing and settlement arrangement for electronic banking and electronic money transfer; linkages between i-banking and e-commerce
6. Any other matter, which the Working Group may think as of relevance to Internet banking in India.

Keeping in view the terms of reference, the Group made a number of recommendations. A summary of these recommendations is given below.

1.8.1 Technology and Security Standards: The role of the network and database administrator is pivotal in securing the information system of any organization. Some of the important functions of the administrator via-a-vis system security are to ensure that only the latest versions of the licensed software with latest patches are installed in the system, proper user groups with access privileges are created and users are assigned to appropriate groups as per their business roles, a proper system of back up of data and software is in place and is strictly adhered to, business continuity plan is in place and frequently tested and there is a robust system of keeping log of all network activity and analyzing the same.

Organizations should make explicit security plan and document it. There should be a separate Security Officer / Group dealing exclusively with information systems security. The Information Technology Division will actually implement the computer systems while the Computer Security Officer will deal with its security. The Information Systems Auditor will audit the information systems.

Access Control: Logical access controls should be implemented on data, systems, application software, utilities, telecommunication lines, libraries, system software, etc. Logical access control techniques may include user-ids, passwords, smart cards or other biometric technologies.

Firewalls: At the minimum, banks should use the proxy server type of firewall so that there is no direct connection between the Internet and the bank's system. It facilitates a high level of control and in-depth monitoring using logging and auditing tools. For sensitive systems, a stateful inspection firewall is recommended which thoroughly inspects all packets of information, and past and present transactions are compared. These generally include a real-time security alert.

Isolation of Dial up Services: All the systems supporting dial up services through modem on the same LAN as the application server should be isolated to prevent intrusions into the network as this may bypass the proxy server.

Security Infrastructure: PKI is the most favoured technology for secure Internet banking services. However, it is not yet commonly available. While PKI infrastructure is strongly recommended, during the transition period, until IDRBT or Government puts in place the PKI infrastructure, the following options are recommended

- Usage of SSL, which ensures server authentication and the use of client side certificates issued by the banks themselves using a Certificate Server.
- The use of at least 128-bit SSL for securing browser to web server communications and, in addition, encryption of sensitive data like passwords in transit within the enterprise itself.

Isolation of Application Servers: It is also recommended that all unnecessary services on the application server such as ftp, telnet should be disabled. The application server should be isolated from the e-mail server.

Security Log (audit Trail): All computer accesses, including messages received, should be logged. All computer access and security violations (suspected or attempted) should be reported and follow up action taken as the organization's escalation policy.

Penetration Testing: The information security officer and the information system auditor should undertake periodic penetration tests of the system, which should include:

- Attempting to guess passwords using password-cracking tools.
- Search for back door traps in the programs.
- Attempt to overload the system using DdoS (Distributed Denial of Service) & DoS (Denial of Service) attacks.
- Check if commonly known holes in the software, especially the browser and the e-mail software exist.
- The penetration testing may also be carried out by engaging outside experts (often called 'Ethical Hackers').

Physical Access Controls: Though generally overlooked, physical access controls should be strictly enforced. The physical security should cover all the information systems and sites where they are housed both against internal and external threats.

Back up and Recovery: The bank should have a proper infrastructure and schedules for backing up data. The backed-up data should be periodically tested to ensure recovery without loss of transactions in a time frame as given out in the bank's security policy. Business continuity should be ensured by having disaster recovery sites, where backed-up data is stored. These facilities should also be tested periodically.

Monitoring against Threats: The banks should acquire tools for monitoring systems and the networks against intrusions and attacks. These tools should be used regularly to avoid security breaches.

Education and Review: The banks should review their security infrastructure and security policies regularly and optimize them in the light of their own experiences and changing technologies. They should educate on a continuous basis their security personnel and also the end-users.

Log of Messages: The banking applications run by the bank should have proper record keeping facilities for legal purposes. It may be necessary to keep all received and sent messages both in encrypted and decrypted form. (When stored in encrypted form, it should be possible to decrypt the information for legal purpose by obtaining keys with owners' consent.)

Certified Products: The banks should use only those security solutions/products which are properly certified for security and for record keeping by independent agencies (such as IDRBT).

Maintenance of Infrastructure: Security infrastructure should be properly tested before using the systems and applications for normal operations. The bank should upgrade the systems by installing patches released by developers to remove bugs and loopholes, and upgrade to newer versions which give better security and control.

Approval for I-banking: All banks having operations in India and intending to offer Internet banking services to public must obtain an approval for the same from RBI. The application for approval should clearly cover the systems and products that the bank plans to use as well as the security plans and infrastructure. It should include sufficient details for RBI to evaluate security, reliability, availability, auditability, recoverability, and other important aspects of the services. RBI may provide model documents for Security Policy, Security Architecture, and Operations Manual.

1.8.2 Legal Issues: The banks providing Internet banking service, at present are only accepting the request for opening of accounts. The accounts are opened only after proper physical introduction and verification. Considering the legal position prevalent, particularly of Section 131 of the Negotiable Instruments Act, 1881 and different case laws, the Group holds the view that there is an obligation on the banks not only to establish the identity but also to make enquiries about integrity and reputation of the prospective customer. The Group, therefore, endorses the present practice but has suggested that after coming in to force of the Information Technology Act, 2000 and digital certification machinery being in place, it may be possible for the banks to rely on digital signature of the introducer. The present legal regime does not set out the parameters as to the extent to which a person can be bound in respect of an electronic instruction purported to have been issued by him. Generally authentication is achieved by security procedure, which involves methods and devices like user-id, password, personal identification number (PIN), code numbers and encryption etc., used to establish authenticity of an instruction. However, from a legal perspective a security procedure needs to be recognized by law as a substitute for signature. In India, the Information Technology Act, 2000, in Section 3(2) provides for a particular technology (viz., the asymmetric crypto system and hash function) as a means of authenticating electronic record. This has raised the doubt whether the law would recognize the existing methods used by banks as valid methods of authentication. The Group holds the view that as in case of other countries, the law should be technology neutral.

In keeping with the view that law should be technology neutral, the Group has recommended that Section 3(2) of the Information Technology Act, 2000 needs to be amended to provide that in addition to the procedure prescribed there in or that may be prescribed by the Central government, a security procedure mutually agreed to by the concerned parties should be recognized as a valid method of authentication of an electronic document/transaction during the transition period. Banks may be allowed to apply for a license to issue digital signature certificate under Section 21 of the Information Technology Act, 2000 and function as certifying authority for facilitating Internet banking. Reserve Bank of India may recommend to Central Government for notifying the business of certifying authority as an approved activity under clause (o) of Section 6(1) of the Banking Regulations Act, 1949.

Section 40A(3) of the Income Tax Act, 1961 recognizes only payments through a crossed cheque or crossed bank draft, where such payment exceeds Rs. 20000/-, for the purpose of deductible expenses. Since the primary intention of the above provision, which is to prevent tax evasion by ensuring transfer of funds through identified accounts, is also satisfied in case of electronic transfer of funds between accounts, such transfers should also be recognized under the above provision. The Income Tax Act, 1961 should be amended suitably. Under the present regime there is an obligation on banks to maintain secrecy and confidentiality of customer's account. In the Internet banking scenario, the risk of banks not meeting the above obligation is high on account of several factors like customers not being careful about their passwords, PIN and other personal identification details and divulging the same to others, banks' sites being hacked despite all precautions and information accessed by inadvertent finders.

Banks offering Internet banking are taking all reasonable security measures like SSL access, 128 bit encryption, firewalls and other net security devices, etc. The Group is of the view that despite all reasonable precautions, banks will be exposed to enhanced risk of liability to customers on account of breach of secrecy, denial of service etc., because of hacking/ other technological failures. The banks should, therefore, institute adequate risk control measures to manage such risk. In Internet banking scenario there is very little scope for the banks to act on stop-payment instructions from the customers. Hence, banks should clearly notify to the customers the timeframe and the circumstances in which any stop-payment instructions could be accepted.

The banks providing Internet banking service and customers availing of the same are currently entering into agreements defining respective rights and liabilities in respect of Internet banking transactions. A standard format/minimum consent requirement to be adopted by banks may be designed by the Indian Banks' Association, which should capture all essential conditions to be fulfilled by the banks, the customers and relative rights and liabilities arising there from. This will help in standardizing documentation as also develop standard practice among bankers offering Internet banking facility.

The concern that Internet banking transactions may become a conduit for money laundering, has been addressed by the Group. Such transactions are initiated and concluded between designated accounts. Further, the proposed Prevention of Money Laundering Bill 1999 imposes obligation on every banking company to maintain records of transactions for certain prescribed period. The Banking Companies (Period of Preservation of Records) Rules, 1985 also require banks to preserve certain records for a period ranging between 5 to 8 years. The Group is of the view that these legal provisions which are applicable to all banking transactions, whether Internet banking or traditional banking, will adequately take care of this concern and no specific measures for Internet banking is necessary.

The Consumer Protection Act, 1986 defines the rights of consumers in India and is applicable to banking services as well. Currently, the rights and liabilities of customers availing of Internet banking services are being determined by bilateral agreements between the banks and customers. It is open to debate whether any bilateral agreement defining customers rights and liabilities, which are adverse to consumers than what is enjoyed by them in the traditional banking scenario will be legally tenable. Considering the banking practice and rights enjoyed by customers in traditional banking, it appears the banks providing I-banking may not absolve themselves from liability to the customers on account of unauthorized transfer through hacking. Similar position may obtain in case of denial of service. Even though, The Information Technology Act, 2000 has provided for penalty for denial of access to a computer system (Section-43) and hacking (Section – 66), the liability of banks in such situations is not clear. The Group was of the view that the banks providing Internet banking may assess the risk and insure themselves against such risks.

The Information Technology Act, 2000, in Section 72 has provided for penalty for breach of privacy and confidentiality. Further, Section 79 of the Act has also provided for exclusion of liability of a network service provider for data travelling through their network subject to certain conditions. Thus, the liability of banks for breach of privacy when data is travelling through network is not clear. This aspect needs detailed legal examination. The issue of ownership of transactional data stored in banks' computer systems also needs further examination.

1.8.3 Regulatory and Supervisory Issues: All banks, which propose to offer transactional services on the Internet should obtain approval from RBI prior to commencing these services. Bank's application for such permission should indicate its business plan, analysis of cost and benefit, operational arrangements like technology adopted, business partners and third party service providers and systems and control procedures the bank proposes to adopt for managing risks, etc. The bank should also submit a security policy covering recommendations made in chapter-6 of this report and a certificate from an independent auditor that the minimum requirements prescribed there have been met. After the initial approval the banks will be obliged to inform RBI any material changes in the services/products offered by them.

RBI may require banks to periodically obtain certificates from specialist external auditors certifying their security control and procedures. The banks will report to RBI every breach or failure of security systems and procedure and the latter, at its discretion, may decide to commission special audit / inspection of such banks.

To a large extent the supervisory concerns on Internet banking are the same as those of electronic banking in general. The guidelines issued by RBI on 'Risks and Controls in Computers and Telecommunications' will equally apply to Internet banking. The RBI as supervisor would cover the entire risks associated with electronic banking as a part of its regular inspections of banks and develop the requisite expertise for such inspections. Till such capability is built up, RBI may outsource this function to qualified EDP auditors.

Record maintenance and their availability for inspection and audit is a major supervisory focus. RBI's guidelines on 'Preservation and Record Maintenance' will need to be updated to include risks heightened by banking on the net. The enhancements will include access to electronic record only by authorized officials, regular archiving of data, a sufficiently senior officer to be in charge of archived data with well defined responsibilities, use of proper software platform and tools to prevent unauthorized alteration of archived data, availability of data on-line, etc. If not available on-line, the system should be capable of making available the data for the same financial year within 24 hours and past data within a period of maximum 48 hours.

Banks should develop outsourcing guidelines to manage effectively, risks arising out of third party service providers such as risks of disruption in service, defective services and personnel of service providers gaining intimate knowledge of banks' systems and misutilising the same, etc. Alternatively, IBA or IDBRT may develop broad guidelines for use of the banking community.

With the increasing popularity of e-commerce, i.e. buying and selling over the Internet, it has become imperative to set up 'Inter-bank Payment Gateways' for settlement of such transactions. The Group have suggested a protocol for transactions between the customer, the bank and the portal and have recommended a framework for setting up of payment gateways. In their capacity as regulator of banks and payment systems of the country, the RBI should formulate norms for eligibility of an institution to set up a payment gateway and the eligible institution should seek RBI's approval for setting up the same.

Only institutions who are members of the cheque clearing system in the country may be permitted to participate in Inter-bank payment gateways for Internet payment. Each gateway must nominate a bank as the clearing bank to settle all transactions. Only direct debits and credits to accounts maintained with the participating banks by parties to an e-commerce transaction may be routed through a payment gateway. Payments effected using credit cards, payments arising out of cross border e-commerce transactions and all intra-bank payments (i.e. transactions involving only one bank) should be excluded for settlement through an inter-bank payment gateway.

Inter-bank payment gateways must have capabilities for both net and gross settlement. All settlement should be intra-day and as far as possible, in real time. It must be obligatory for payment gateways to maintain complete trace of any payment transaction covering such details like date and time of origin of transaction, payee, payer and a unique transaction reference number (TRN).

Connectivity between the gateway and the computer system of the member bank should be achieved using a leased line network (not through Internet) with appropriate data encryption standard. All transactions must be authenticated using user-id and password. Once, the regulatory framework is in place, the transactions should be digitally certified by any licensed certifying agency. SSL/128 bit encryption must be used as minimum level of security. Adequate firewalls and related security measures must be taken to ensure privacy to the participating institutions in a payment gateway. Internationally accepted standards such as ISO8583 must be used for transmitting payment and settlement messages over the network.

The RBI may have a panel of auditors who will be required to certify the security of the entire infrastructure both at the payment gateway end and the participating institutions end prior to making the facility available for customers use. The credit risk associated with each payment transaction will be on the payee bank. The legal basis for such transactions and settlement will be the bilateral contracts between the payee and payee's bank, the participating banks and service provider and the banks themselves. The rights and obligations of each party must be clearly stated in the mandate and should be valid in a court of law.

It will be necessary to make customers aware of risks inherent in doing business over the Internet. This requirement will be met by making mandatory disclosures of risks, responsibilities and liabilities to the customers through a disclosure template. The banks should also provide their latest published financial results over the net.

Hyperlinks from banks' websites, often raise the issue of reputational risk. Such links should not mislead the customers in to believing that they sponsor any particular product or any business unrelated to banking. Hence, hyperlinks from a bank's websites should be confined to only those portals with which they have a payment arrangement or sites of their subsidiaries or principals. Hyperlinks to banks' website from different portals are normally meant to pass information pertaining to purchases made by banks' customers in the portal. Banks must follow the minimum recommended security precautions while dealing with such request, which includes customer authentication through user-id and password, independent confirmation of transaction by the customer and authorizing payment, use of SSL and 128 bit encryption for all communication both with the portal and customer browser terminal, etc.

On the question of additional capital charge on banks, which undertake Internet banking, the group held the view that standards have not yet been developed for measuring additional capital charge for operational risk. However, this requirement could be covered as the RBI moves towards risk based supervision.

The applicability of various existing laws and banking practices to E-banking is not tested and is still in the process of evolving, both in India and abroad. With rapid changes in technology and innovation in the field of E-banking, there is a need for constant review of different laws relating to banking and commerce. The Group, therefore, recommends that the Reserve Bank of India may constitute a multi disciplinary high level standing committee to review the legal and technological requirements of E-banking on continual basis and recommend appropriate measures as and when necessary.

The regulatory and supervisory framework for E-banking is continuing to evolve and the regulatory authorities all over the world recognize the need for cooperative approach in this area. The Basle Committee for Banking Supervision (BCBS) has constituted an Electronic Banking Group (EBG) to develop guiding principles for the prudent risk management of E-banking activities. This Working Group, therefore, recommends that the Reserve Bank of India should maintain close contact with regulating/supervisory authorities of different countries as well as with the Electronic Banking Group of BCBS and review its regulatory framework in keeping with developments elsewhere in the world.

The Group submitted its report in June 2001 and the Reserve Bank while accepting the recommendations of the Working Group, issued guidelines on 'Internet Banking in India' for implementation by banks. It also stated that the earlier guidelines issued by the Reserve Bank on 'Risks and Controls in Computers and Telecommunications' (1998) would equally apply to Internet banking as well.

1.9 E-banking Challenges and Concerns

E-banking is based on technology that by its very nature is designed to expand the "virtual" geographic reach of banks and customers without necessarily requiring a similar "physical" expansion. Such market expansion can extend beyond national borders which significantly increases cross-border cooperation challenges for bank supervisors due to:

- The potential ease and speed with which banks located anywhere in the world can conduct activities with customers over interconnected electronic networks4 into countries where a bank is not licensed or supervised.
- The potential ability of a bank or non-bank to use the Internet to cross borders and to seamlessly link banking activities that have typically been subject to supervision with non-banking activities that might be unsupervised by any financial market authority.
- The practical difficulties faced by national authorities wishing to monitor or control local access to E-banking sites originating in other jurisdictions without the cooperation of home country authorities.

Banking organisations have been delivering services to consumers and businesses remotely for years. Electronic funds transfer, including small payments and corporate cash management systems, as well as publicly accessible machines for currency withdrawal and retail account management are global fixtures. However, delivering financial services over public networks such as the Internet is bringing about a fundamental shift in the financial services industry.

The changes created, and some of the technical characteristics of internet technology raise new concerns for both bankers and supervisors. Banking organisations are focusing increasingly on their E-banking activities and are globally expanding Internet banking activities, exploring the use of wireless networks and venturing into some new areas of electronic commerce.

Banks offer E-banking services to defend or expand market share or as a cost saving strategy to reduce paperwork and personnel. The Internet also provides banks with substantial opportunity to extend their customer reach beyond existing boundaries. However, the nature of the open network and the evolution of electronic commerce exposes banks to significant competition from both banking and non-banking firms. In addition, electronic delivery channels operate in an uncertain legal and regulatory environment that differs by jurisdiction.

All these factors present new challenges for financial institutions in managing security, integrity and availability of services provided while remaining sufficiently profitable.

Following are the emerging trends and issues that could impact bank risk profiles:

1. A significant increase in competition in the electronic financial services industry as both banking and non-banking firms rapidly introduce new financial products and services.
2. Rapid technological improvements in telecommunications and computer hardware and software enabling greater speed in transactions processing.
3. Bank management and staff often lack expertise in technology and E-banking risk issues.
4. Greater reliance on outsourcing to third party service providers, and a proliferation of new alliances and joint ventures with non-financial firms.
5. Greater demand for global infrastructures for technology that are scalable, flexible and interoperable, both within and across enterprises and that can ensure the security, integrity and availability of information and services.
6. Increased potential for fraud, due to the absence of standard business practices for customer verification and authentication on open networks like the Internet.
7. Legal and regulatory ambiguity and uncertainty with respect to the application and jurisdiction of current laws and regulations to evolving E-banking activities.
8. The collection, storage and frequent sharing of significant quantities of customer data can lead to customer privacy issues that potentially create prudential risks for banks (e.g. legal and reputational).
9. Questions regarding the effectiveness and efficiency of online disclosures. Lengthy or complicated online disclosures may cause customers to simply "click through" or even quit a web

site; moreover, extensive disclosure reduces the speed at which web sites and pages can be downloaded.

Banks and bank supervisors generally agree that the supervisory principles that apply to traditional banking are applicable to E-banking. However, the combination of rapid changes in technology and the degree of bank dependence on technology vendors and service providers modify and sometimes magnify traditional risks. Hence, there is a need for additional supervisory guidance in selected areas to enhance the overall risk management framework for E-banking activities.

These developments in E-banking to date suggest that:

- The desire to benefit from the advantages of e-commerce in financial services has become widespread. The financial services industry is increasingly focused on providing technology-based financial services solutions directly to customers in order to help build and retain customer bases.
- Speed-to-market has become a critical factor for success in E-banking. To reduce time to market, banking institutions are allying with non-banking firms to provide total financial services solutions.
- The current trends in the formation of strategic alliances and technology outsourcing will grow.

These developments present challenges for both banks and bank supervisors. Bank management needs to re-evaluate the robustness of traditional risk management practices in light of the new risks posed by E-banking activities. Also, bank supervisors need to take a balanced approach to the introduction of new regulation and supervisory policy on E-banking, so as to ensure safe and sound operations of banks while at the same time not stifling innovation and the competitiveness of the banks relative to non-banks.

1.10 E-banking Risks and Their Management

E-banking using the Internet as an added delivery channel may shift bank risk profiles to some degree and create new risk control challenges for banks. Accordingly, bank supervisors need to consider the implications of a bank's use of the E-banking delivery channel on its strategic risk, operational risk, reputational risk, legal risk, credit risk, liquidity risk, market risk and foreign exchange risk.

1.10.1 Strategic and Business Risk: Strategic risk is one of the most significant risks that E-banking activities present for banking organisations. Strategic risk differs from other risk categories in that it is more general and broad in nature. Strategic decisions to be taken by a bank's Board of Directors and executive management will have implications for all other risk categories.

Given growing customer acceptance and demand for E-banking, as well as the potential efficiencies afforded, most banks will need to develop a strategy to use the Internet delivery channel to provide informational content and/or transactional service to customers. The rapid changes in technology, the pace of competition with other banks and non-bank competitors and the nature of that strategy could expose banks to substantial risk if the planning and implementation of the strategy is flawed or otherwise not well thought through.

Some of the strategic risks involved with E-banking are directly linked with timing issues. There can be significant strategic risk associated with a management decision to be a technology pioneer, particularly if the institution becomes burdened with systems made redundant by rapid technological changes. Likewise, an overly cautious technology follower may find itself unable to adequately position itself in a saturated market or a market that is consolidating rapidly.

Prior to the Internet, banking institutions used proprietary networks within their consolidated enterprise and connected in limited ways to other banks. These proprietary networks helped provide a strategic defence against new entrants and provided individual franchise protection. However, the Internet as an open network with open access allows both banks and non-banks freedom to create and leverage existing business without the need for expanded physical presence. Consequently, competition within the financial services industry has been significantly increased and is likely to increase further.

Most bankers believe that the E-banking delivery channel will enable them to reduce operational expenses. However, many bank customers wish to maintain a traditional banking relationship, which makes it difficult for banks to abandon the existing physical infrastructure. This means that banks will - at least for the foreseeable future - need to run multiple delivery channels for sometime and E-banking will be a net additional expense. Thus, operational expense savings may occur over the long run only.

The challenge the banking industry faces in maintaining market share is complicated by the entry of new firms that are providing individual financial services via the Internet to existing bank customers. The emergence of aggregation and screen scraping technologies poses both strategic opportunities and threats to banks. Depending on the evolving relationship between the aggregator, the banks affected and the consumer, banks may get further disintermediated as aggregators potentially disrupt the traditional relationship between the customer and the bank and "limit" the direct access that banks will have on-line to retail customers. In addition, aggressive aggregation by both banks and non-banks may lead to greater commoditisation of banking products and services, thereby reducing bank profit margins and adding new security and legal risks.

In essence, bank management needs to carefully consider how its Internet strategy will help maintain the competitiveness and profitability of the institution yet not lead to unwarranted increases in its risk profile. Supervisors should expect banking institutions to carefully assess the pros and cons associated with their strategic options.

1.10.2 Operational Risk: Because of the reliance on technology for all facets of E-banking, operational risk is one of the more significant risks. To limit operational risk, banking organisations may want to consider implementing an integrated enterprise-wide architecture and technology infrastructure that can facilitate interoperability, ensure the security, integrity and availability of data and support the management of relationships with third-party service providers. Further, as technology is also dramatically changing business models and operating processes, banks need to ensure that they have appropriate control procedures (including change control) and audit processes.

A. Technology Infrastructure: E-banking has brought the issue of technological systems and applications integration to the forefront. Many large banks are now faced with the task of integrating systems for E-banking activities with their existing legacy systems and with the systems of multiple service providers and partners. These banks are exposed to significant operational risks from errors in transaction processing if the systems for E-banking are not properly integrated.

Accordingly, many large banks are making significant investments in technology infrastructure in order to create improved internal controls and enhanced risk management oversight processes. The banks are also hoping to improve flexibility, scalability and interoperability of their systems and operations both within their enterprises and across outside service providers.

While these general developments by large banks are positive, in general the banking industry has much further to go towards improving its systems and risk management infrastructure to effectively support E-banking. Small to medium-sized banking organisations are particularly challenged because of budget restrictions for acquiring hardware and software, as well as attracting and keeping technical staff. Many of these banks rely significantly on third party service providers to manage the necessary technological infrastructure to support the bank's E-banking operations. In this situation, the bank still retains ultimate responsibility for ensuring that these operations are well controlled and managed, and the bank supervisor will wish to assess the ongoing ability of bank management to do so adequately.

B. Security: The majority of bankers surveyed by EBG members identified security risk as a primary concern relating to

E-banking. External threats such as "hacking" [5], "sniffing" [6], "spoofing" [7] and "denial of service" [8] attacks expose banks to new security risks. Open electronic delivery channels create new security issues for banks with respect to confidentiality and integrity of information, non-repudiation of transactions, authentication of users and access control.

Most banks appear to be sensitive to external security threats. Among the issues identified for immediate attention is the development of more robust tools to verify the identity and authenticity of larger value transaction requests. [9] In addition, the banking industry needs to continue to work towards international best practices for encryption requirements, including the legality of electronic signature and records. Moreover, since many banks' internal networks rely on security technology similar to that used to manage their external systems, it is important that bankers also be sensitive to managing the security risk arising from their internal networks. If not managed properly, internal security exposures can also compromise the integrity and confidentiality of bank records and customer data. [10]

Poor security may create reputational or legal risks for banks, as they may be deemed to have provided inappropriate protection for customers' personal data, with consequential legal and/or reputational damage.

At the international level, bank supervisors should encourage the development of a comprehensive approach to managing risk associated with both internal and external security exposures. Given the continuing evolution of industry standards, security risk management may be an area where bank supervisors can work collaboratively with the industry to promote the development of sound practices.

C. Data Integrity: Data integrity is an important component of system security. Banking organisations must improve interoperability within and across enterprises to effectively manage relationships with customers, other banks and external service providers. Until industry standards are identified for electronic data management, banking organisations will continue to be challenged to establish effective control processes to ensure the accuracy and integrity of data being transmitted and received. The processes should include, at a minimum, sound policies and practices related to project management, system development life cycle, change control and quality assurance. Bank supervisors should also encourage banks to review the integrity of the data used by their risk management systems.

Given the lower cost and ubiquitous nature of the Internet, organisations are increasingly using TCP/IP [11] as a standard communications protocol to achieve this. While there are significant benefits of communicating via TCP/IP, organisations must ensure that data transmitted between bank legacy systems and systems of other parties are translated and integrated accurately. Moreover, while the introduction of middleware [12] and languages such as XML [13] are helping to facilitate this effort, the development of industry standards to support these new technologies is still in its very early stages.

D. System Availability: In addition to ensuring a secure internal network for their E-banking activities, effective capacity planning is critical to ensuring the ongoing availability of E-banking products and services. Transaction volumes may become increasingly volatile due to price sensitivities and greater automation. Also, competitive pressures and increased reliance on having services available 24 hours a day and 7 days a week (24x7) have raised customer expectations considerably and in turn reduced the tolerance for error. To compete effectively and avoid potentially significant reputation risk that could arise from systems outages, banks offering E-banking services must deliver the right mix of products and services securely, accurately and consistently. These factors underscore the importance of effective business continuity, recovery and incident response plans. Moreover, trends in outsourcing make it necessary for bankers to ensure that similar plans are in place at their external service providers and are periodically tested for effectiveness.

Denials of service attacks can also reduce or eliminate a bank's ability to serve its customers while under attack. These attacks have become increasingly common against high profile e-commerce providers. An added challenge is posed by banks' inability to control the availability of the Internet network itself. Thus, a bank needs to consider, as part of its contingency plans, alternative means to deliver service in the event of a major disruption to the Internet network.

E. Internal Controls/Audit: The ability to detect and correct errors is a critical internal control component of any banking operation. Moreover, banking organisations must have sufficient controls in place to prevent fraud from both internal and external sources and safeguard the bank's information and assets.

Much of the efficiency and cost reduction in E-banking services stem from banks' ability to implement "straight-through processing". [14] While the benefits of straight-through processing are many, the reality is that E-banking modifies how internal controls, proper segregation of duties and clear audit trails are applied over broad access channels. The challenges presented by these changes are compounded by a critical shortage of skills and expertise in the industry in both the operations and audit areas. Going forward, banks will be increasingly challenged to ensure that highly automated environments provide effective control and that the controls can be independently audited.

F. Outsourcing: Perhaps more than any other industry development relating to E-banking, banks' increased reliance on outsourcing is having a significant impact on the risk profiles of all banking organisations – both large and small. Large banks are outsourcing many activities as they are increasingly focusing on their core businesses and partnering with other organisations for solutions outside of their core competencies. Small banks usually must outsource because they often lack the necessary technical expertise and resources to build an E-banking delivery channel on their own. Additionally, a decline in the cost of "turnkey" solutions has made it more affordable for small banks to purchase E-banking applications from vendors. These developments are positive in that they increase efficiency, they allow smaller institutions to compete more effectively and they promote the introduction of "state of the art" applications within the industry. However, they can also substantially add to banks' challenges in managing operational risk.

Preliminary indications from surveys tend to indicate that financial institutions rely upon a relatively small number of third-party providers. This seems to be especially the case for small to medium-sized institutions. In some cases, these third parties happen to be new firms with a relatively short track record. This apparent reliance on a concentrated number of third parties, which the EBG will investigate further, could have systemic implications if a major problem would arise with one of these service providers.

To properly manage the risks associated with outsourcing, banks must conduct appropriate due diligence and monitoring of the ongoing viability of third party service providers. The adequacy of terms under contract and service level agreements must also be carefully reviewed for legal risk. Operations processing and the management of security, integrity and availability risks are also more complicated. Furthermore, many technology providers and partners are newly established and may lack knowledge of the controls required within a banking environment. Minor disruptions on the part of third party service providers can expose banking organisations to potential financial loss and substantial legal and reputation risk. Complexity is also added by multiple vendor/service provider relationships that often support E-banking operations. Although to date such disruptions seem to have been controlled, in the future their potential impact could be quite considerable and raises significant concerns for supervisors and industry participants.

Outsourcing can lead to additional privacy related risk exposures. Banks may not always be aware of the exact collection and usage of customer data by vendors and other third parties, and/or may not be adequately managing such activities. Moreover, the legal rights and responsibilities of service providers and vendors may not always be clear. Banks should be encouraged to address privacy issues in their contractual and ongoing relations with vendors.

Various bank supervisors around the world have developed specific guidance related to technology outsourcing. The EBG plans to conduct a review of such guidance and to explore ways to coordinate the development of sound practices in this area for both the banking industry and its supervisors.

1.10.3 Reputational Risk: A bank's reputation can be impacted by any adverse development that precludes the availability of their E-banking delivery channel. Banks have long based their business on a reputation of trust. The ability to provide a trusted network to support E-banking is critical, and a bank's reputation can be damaged by Internet banking services that are poorly executed or otherwise alienate customers and the public.

A bank's reputation can suffer if it fails to deliver secure, accurate and timely E-banking services on a consistent basis. A bank's reputation can also be adversely impacted if it fails to respond to inquiries posted via e-mail, does not provide proper disclosure, or violates customer privacy.

Hypertext links from a bank to third party web sites or outsourced service providers may cause customer confusion about the provider of specific products and services offered, and whether they are insured or uninsured. Customers can also be confused about whether the links from the bank reflect an implied endorsement of the third party's products or services and may well look to the bank for recourse if problems are encountered.

Further, major security breaches in a bank or a non-bank competitor's web site could undermine overall consumer or market confidence in banks' ability to appropriately manage Internet-based transactions.

Any problems that a bank might experience with regard to data and privacy protection could threaten the reputation of that bank as well as the reputation of any other banks perceived to be involved in similar activities.

To protect against adverse situations that may cause damage to their reputation, banking organisations should develop and monitor performance standards for their E-banking activities. Regular review and testing of business continuity, recovery and incident response plans, and communications strategies are also critical to protecting banks' reputations.

1.10.4 Legal Risk: Legal risk arising from E-banking activities represents another area of increased concern. Currently, supervisors in every jurisdiction are examining how existing legal and regulatory frameworks originally designed to address issues affecting the "physical' world of banking interact with the developing E-banking delivery channel as well as examining potential ambiguities.

A bank that develops relationships via the Internet with customers in other jurisdictions may be unfamiliar with the banking and customer protection laws and regulations specific to those countries and may consequently incur heightened legal risks. Even banks that do not intend to solicit business from consumers in foreign jurisdictions may find that their offerings on-line are considered solicitations in some countries. For example, if a bank makes its web site available in another language, regulators in any country where that language is spoken may determine that the bank is marketing services to its citizens and may find that the bank is therefore subject to its local laws and regulations.

Unauthorised use or misuse of data collected over the Internet is another potential source of legal risk. Unauthorised individuals can attack and/or try to infiltrate the "data warehouses" [15] maintained about consumers by both banks and third party vendors. For example, hackers or others might break into banks' or vendors' databases or build their own databases and use the consumers' information to perpetrate fraud. Authorised staff may also deliberately misuse data. Surveys of banks and third party vendors conducted by the EBG have showed that such attacks on "data warehouses" have already occurred, although the impact of these attacks has been minimal to date.

The enforceability of certain emerging areas of law is also uncertain. Laws related to the enforceability of electronic contracts and digital signatures are still under development and vary from jurisdiction to jurisdiction. Effective "know your customer" (KYC) practices are also becoming more critical to bankers in their attempts to prevent fraud.

1.10.5 Other Traditional Banking Risks: The E-banking delivery channel also has implications for other traditional banking risks such as credit risk, liquidity risk, interest rate risk, and market risks. The impact of the introduction of E-banking does not necessarily result in an increase or decrease in the risk profile of the institution, but risks can be shifted, sometimes in complex ways.

A. Credit Risk: The credit risk of a banking institution can be affected by E-banking activities in a number of ways. The use of the Internet delivery channel may allow banks, especially small institutions, to expand very rapidly, which could lead to heightened asset quality and internal control risks. The use of the Internet also allows banks to expand their geographic reach out of their traditional area, which increases the challenge of understanding local market dynamics and risks, verifying collateral and perfecting security liens with out-of-area borrowers. In addition, the Internet also makes it more difficult to authenticate the identity and creditworthiness of a potential customer, which are essential elements to sound credit decisions. [16] Further, there has been a tendency for some Internet-only banks to pay higher rates on deposits opened over the Internet, which could lead to a higher level of sub-prime credits at these institutions in order to support these higher deposit rates. These factors underscore the importance of sound credit underwriting policies, credit monitoring and administration practices regardless of which product delivery channel is used.

B. Liquidity Risk: The speed with which information and misinformation moves over the Internet can have implications for the liquidity risk profile of a bank. Adverse information about a bank, whether it is true or not, can be easily disseminated over the Internet through bulletin boards and news groups. This could cause depositors to withdraw their funds in mass at any time of the day, any day of the week. Also, Internet banking can increase deposit volatility to the extent that new customers brought in through this channel maintain accounts solely on the basis of interest rate or terms. Accordingly, increased monitoring of liquidity and changes in deposits and loans may be warranted depending on the volume of activity created through E-banking.

C. Market Risk: The impact of recent growth in securities issuance and trading over the Internet on banks' market risk profiles is complex. From a market standpoint, the increased volume of securities, which are traded over the Internet, can on the one hand lead to increased volatility, but, on the other hand, it can lead to increased liquidity. From an individual bank's standpoint, banks may be exposed to increased market risk if they create or expand deposit brokering, loan sales, or securitisation programme as a result of Internet banking activities. As with liquidity risk, the effects of increased E-banking activities on market volatility need to be monitored by banks and supervisors.

D. Foreign Exchange Risk: A bank may be exposed to foreign exchange risk if it accepts deposits from foreign customers or create accounts denominated in currencies other than their local currency. Since the Internet allows banks the opportunity to expand their geographic range, even internationally, some banks may take on greater foreign exchange risk through E-banking activities than they have through their traditional delivery channels. Also, foreign exchange risk can be intensified by political, social or economic developments, which a bank inexperienced in cross-border banking may not appreciate fully. Supervisors should ensure that a bank initiating cross-border E-banking activities through the Internet has the appropriate risk management systems and expertise to manage these risks properly.

As the preceding discussion indicates, the basic types of risks associated with E-banking are not new. However, the specific ways in which these risks arise, as well as the potential magnitude and speed of impact on banks, may be new for bank management and supervisors alike. In addition, while assessing risk should already be dynamic, the rapid pace of technological innovation supporting E-banking, the increased degree of systems outsourcing and the reliance of some products/services on the use of open networks such as the Internet, intensifies the need for a rigorous and ongoing risk management process.

Bank supervisors should expect their banks to have comprehensive risk management processes in place that include the three basic elements of *assessing* risks, *controlling* risk exposure, and *monitoring* risks associated with E-banking. This comprehensive risk management framework should be integrated into the bank's overall risk management framework.

It is also essential that this risk management process is supported by appropriate oversight by the board of directors and senior management and is carried out by staff with the necessary knowledge and skills to deal with the technical complexities of new E-banking developments.

Similarly, bank supervisors must recognise their own critical need for supervisory staff with appropriate technology knowledge and skills to ensure that they understand the risks and challenges arising from the development of the E-banking delivery channel. Enhanced technical training of existing supervisory staff, complemented by appropriate recruitment of outside expertise, should be a high priority in order to ensure that the supervisor keeps abreast of increasingly complex technology and market developments.

1.11 Electronic Money (E-Money)

In recent years, there has been a gradual switchover from the use of paper-based payments media to those based on electronics. While the basic characteristics of these new instruments are by and large similar to those of paper-based instruments, the former present a different set of challenges to policy makers. Electronic money (e-money) is one such new product which has appeared on Indian horizon recently.

1.11.1 Meaning of E-Money: E-money may be broadly defined as an electronic store of monetary value on a technical device used for making payments to undertakings other than the issuer without necessarily involving bank accounts in the transaction, but acting as a prepaid bearer instrument. These products could be classified into two broad categories, viz. (a) pre-paid stored value card (sometimes called "electronic purse") and (b) pre-paid software based product that uses computer networks such as internet (sometimes referred to as "digital cash" or "network money"). The stored value card scheme typically uses a microprocessor chip embedded in a plastic card while software based scheme typically uses specialised software installed in a personal computer.

1.11.2 Recommendations of the Working Group on Electronic Money (Chairman: Zarir J. Cama), 2002: In January 2002, the RBI constituted a Working Group on Electronic Money which submitted its report in July 2002. The Group identified certain areas of concern from the point of view of the central bank in the context of more widespread use of e-money so that the conduct of monetary policy is not impaired and at the same time, the integrity of the instrument is also preserved. Some of the suggestions made by the Group included (a) multi-purpose e-money to be issued only by authorised banks on a credit basis, which should be strictly regulated and closely monitored, (b) ensure redeemability in order to preserve the unit of account function of money as well as to control money supply in the economy and (c) reporting of monetary statistics for the purposes of monetary policy and protection against criminal abuse, such as money laundering.

Summary and recommendations of the Report are set forth below.

Broadly, e-money is an electronic store of monetary value on a technical device. E-money could be classified as (a) pre-paid stored value card (sometimes called "electronic purse") and (b) pre-paid software based product that uses computer networks such as internet (sometimes referred to as "digital cash" or "network money"). The stored value card could be of three types - single-purpose card, closed-system or limited-purpose card and general-purpose or multi-purpose card. The single-purpose card generally with a magnetic chip recording the amount of fund therein is designed to facilitate only one type of transaction e.g., telephone calls, public transportation, laundry, parking facilities etc. Here, the distinguishing point is that the issuer and the service provider (acceptor) are identical for such cards. The closed-system or the limited-purpose cards are generally used in a small number of well-identified points of sale within a well-identified location such as corporate/university campus. The multi-purpose card on the other can perform variety of functions with several vendors viz., credit card, debit card, stored value card, identification card, repository of personal medical information etc.

While it may not be desirable place any limit on storing monetary value in e-money, it is expected that e-money could be used to substitute central bank notes and coins at least partially. However, the importance of e-money with respect to regulatory oversight, restrictions on issuers and their implications for monetary policy is extremely critical from the point of view of the central bank.

After considering various issues, the Group recommends that multi-purpose e-money may be permitted to be issued only against payment of full value of central bank money or against credit only by the banks. The issuance of e-money on credit basis should, however, be strictly regulated and closely monitored.

It needs to be appreciated that issuers must be under obligation to offer redemption of their e-money liabilities net of service charges, if so required. From monetary policy point of view, such redemption requirement is essential in order to preserve unit of account function of money as also to control money supply in the economy.

With regard to status of issuers of e-money, it may be indicated that there are five reasons which may warrant banks as the issuers of multi-purpose e-money. These include attributes of e-money being closure to demand liabilities of the bank, implications of e-money on velocity of circulation of money and its corresponding impact on monetary statistics, the option to impose reserve requirement on e-money, the need for closure monitoring of e-money when these would be issued as credit and the technical security of e-money. For all these reasons, the Group recommends that only banks should be allowed to issue multi-purpose e-money. However, single-purpose and limited-purpose e-money should be allowed to be issued by any entity including banks.

Non-banks should not be permitted to issue multi-purpose e-money. If they are permitted, they along with banks must conform to seven minimum prudential requirements as laid down by European Central Bank (ECB) in 1998. These are (i) prudential supervision of issuers of e-money by the central bank, (ii) solid and transparent legal arrangements codifying the rights and obligations of issuers, merchants, consumers and the regulators, (iii) adequate technical, organisational and procedural safeguards to prevent and detect threats to the security of e-money, (iv) protection against criminal abuse, (v) supplying of all relevant information to the central bank for the purpose of monetary policy, (vi) legal obligations to redeem e-money against central bank money at par at the request of the holder and (vii) the right of the central bank to impose reserve requirement on issuers of e-money.

E-money could have profound impact on compilation of monetary statistics and money supply unless regulated prudently. E-money could be issued against cash (i.e., 100 per cent backed by central bank money paid upfront). Since e-money are close substitutes of central bank money, these should be explicitly accounted for in monetary statistics. If e-money is allowed to be issued only by banks, then currency would be substituted with demand/time liabilities through e-money. In that eventually, issuance of e-money would be money stock neutral and no change would be required in the definition of money stock. However, if e-money is issued by entities other than depository institutions (i.e. banks), the money creating sector as embedded in compilation of monetary statistics would need to be broadened.

There could be a situation where residents could use e-money supplied by entities outside the country for domestic transactions. In that case, monetary aggregates would lose its predictive power. 48. It is expected that the proportion of interest bearing liabilities in monetary aggregates would grow in the event of growing use of e-money which would render them more unstable, and information content of monetary aggregates would also change.

If e-money is issued on credit, there is a possibility that the issuers may assume a leveraged position. There is, therefore, a need for continuous monitoring of the behaviour of issuing authorities for balanced growth of their assets and liabilities, particularly liabilities arising out of issuance of e-money. For these reasons, the Group recommends that the central bank should regulate and closely monitor the practice of issuing e-money on credit.

If consumers prefer to use e-money vis-a-vis currency, then for a given stock of currency, the money multiplier would go up which would in turn increase the aggregate money supply in the economy more than what would have been the case without e-money. Also, with large scale use of e-money, it has been apprehended that central bank's balance sheet may shrink to such an extent relative to that of the banking sector that it may be unable to perform its liquidity absorption function on account of non-availability of adequate volume of assets. Apart from constraining its liquidity management function, relative shrinkage in balance sheet may also have serious implications regarding loss of *seigniorage* revenue for the central bank. As a counter argument, it is maintained that there should always be a lower bound below which the use of currency notes and coins should not go down so that there should also be a limit below which reserve money should not shrink relative to broad money stock.

A review of developments indicate that while considerations of potential benefits of micro-economic efficiency, extension of banking to urban poor and rural communities and facilitation of e-governance demand that there should be increasingly private provision of payment and settlement services in the economy in future, macro-economic stabilisation policy warrants that there should be a case for public regulation over such provision. Also, currency uses are characterised by network externalities in that larger the number of users, larger is the settlement value of the currency concerned implying that currency could at best be supplied oligopolistically. There are, in fact, the fundamental reasons for which the "monopoly right" in the issuance of currency should be in the hands of some public authority, preferably the central bank. Even then, there cannot be any final judgement on this issue at this point of time. In view of all these considerations, the Group, therefore, recommends that the RBI should regularly monitor closely all these developments so that integrity of the financial system is preserved.

The RBI should also periodically review issues relating to legal framework, if any, technical security and the clearing and settlement arrangements of different e-money schemes and the practices of various e-money schemes, both in India and abroad, for preserving integrity of the financial market. On the issue whether entities other than the central bank could issue independent media of exchanges, the Group feels that such a possibility is apparently remote in India at this point of time. However, RBI may continually keep track of these developments for smooth functioning of the financial market.

1.12 Ensuring E-security

No innovation is without challenges and IT is no exception to this rule. The most prominent challenge arising from these innovations relates to the concept of security (Mohan, 2004c). Considering the scope for fraud in the E-banking area and the possibility of contagion, the Reserve Bank as a regulator and supervisor has been proactive in addressing the risks associated with E-banking that could have otherwise undermined the credibility of the Indian banking sector. The Reserve Bank has been promptly addressing issues related to fraud with the use of electronic banking facility. Even after issuing guidelines for a secured E-banking, the Reserve Bank from time to time advises the banks on control mechanisms to combat such frauds. In a recent case of attempt of fraud by a customer while using internet banking facility, the Reserve Bank advised the concerned bank to plug the loopholes and the same was also communicated to other banks so that they remained vigilant and control the misuse of internet banking system.

In India, the legal infrastructure for promoting E-banking has not yet been put in place in a comprehensive manner. India does not have a licensed certifying authority appointed by the Controller of Certifying Authorities to issue digital signature certificates. Also, India is not yet a signatory to the International Cyber Crime Treaty, which seeks to intensify co-operation among different signatory nations for exchanging information concerning crime and cyber criminals. Further, there are unresolved legislative issues related to cyber crimes laws, clarification relating to regulatory authority over e-money products, consumer protection and privacy laws. To make the E-banking operations in India more widespread, secure and efficient, these issues need to be addressed by relevant authorities.

As the banking practices and legislations concerning E-banking are still in the process of evolution in India and abroad because of technological innovations, there is a need for a constant review of various legislations and regulatory framework relating to banking and commerce. The Reserve Bank is monitoring and reviewing the legal and other requirements of E-banking on a continuous basis to ensure that the E-banking would develop on sound lines and the E-banking related challenges would not pose a threat to financial stability.

Notes

1. Reserve Bank of India, Report on Currency and Finance, 2001-02, p. VI-1.

2. Government of India, Planning Commission, *Ninth Five Year Plan* (1997-2002), Vol. I, p. 150.

3. As the lender of the last resort, the RBI helps the commercial banks in temporary need of cash when other sources of raising cash are exhausted. The RBI provides credit to banks by rediscounting eligible

bills of exchange and by making advances against eligible securities such as government securities. The lending rate for these advances by the RBI is called the bank rate which is a traditional weapon of control money supply. An increase in the bank rate would discourage commercial banks to borrow from the RBI and a corresponding increase in the lending rate of commercial banks to general public would decrease public borrowings from the banks.

4. Reserve Bank of India, Report on Currency and Finance, 2001-02 p. VI-16.

5. Hacking refers to the practice of breaking into a computer without authorisation, for malicious reasons, just to prove it can be done, or for other personal reasons.

6. Sniffing involves the use of a software program that is illicitly inserted somewhere on a network to capture ("sniff") user passwords as they pass through the system.

7. Spoofing refers to an attempt to gain access to a system by posing as an authorised user.

8. A denial of service attack represents an attempt to overwhelm a server with requests so that it cannot respond to legitimate traffic.

9. Identification is concerned with positively establishing the identity of the person or organisation conducting the transaction. Passwords are a common approach although evolving approaches such as biometrics may become increasingly prevalent. Authorisation is concerned with establishing the authority that an individual has to conduct a particular transaction.

10. Attacks on internal systems including those by employees are more frequent than external attacks in many organisations.

11. TCP/IP is a standardised communications protocol for transmitting data in packets via the Internet. TCP (Transfer Control Protocol) deals with the construction of the data packets, while IP (Internet Protocol) routes them from computer to computer.

12. Middleware is transaction-processing software that facilitates client/server communications over a network (e.g. TCP/IP) allowing client applications to access and update information from unlike platforms, databases and mainframes.

13. XML (Extensible Mark-up Language) is a universal, flexible, text-based data format that facilitates structured data interchange on the Web.

14. Straight-through processing refers to automatic transaction processing without any human intervention in the transaction process flow.

15 A data warehouse is a large database of customer transactions, updated regularly, which is used as a source of information for data mining.

16 On the other hand, the use of the Internet delivery channel can potentially lead to a reduction in a bank's concentration of credit to a single local industry, market or geographic region.

2

Universal Banking in India: Strategies for Successful Implementation

S. Ganesan and S. Shanmuga Pria

2.1 Introduction

Economic historians have long emphasized the importance of financial institutions in industrialization. More recently, economists have begun more intensive investigation of the links between financial system structure and real economic outcomes. In theory, the organization of financial institutions partly determines the extent of competition among financial intermediaries, the quantity of financial capital drawn into the financial system, and the distribution of that capital to ultimate uses. The choice between universal and specialized banking may affect interest rates, underwriting costs, and the efficiency of secondary markets in securities.

Furthermore, the presence or absence of formal bank relationships may affect the quality of investments undertaken, strategic decision-making, and even the competitiveness of industry. Particularly since World War II, many economists and historians have argued that German-style universal banks offer advantages for industrial development and economic growth. Universal banking efficiency combined with close relationships between banks and industrial firms, they hypothesize, spurred Germany's rapid development at the end of the nineteenth century and again in the post-World War II reconstruction. A corollary to this view holds that countries that failed to adopt the universal-relationship system suffered as a consequence. Adherents suggest that British industry has declined over the past hundred years or more, and that the American economy has failed to reach its full potential, due to short-comings of the financial system that lead to relatively high costs of capital.

2.2 Indian Banking Scenario

There has been a paradigm shift in mindsets both at the Government level and at the policy framing level in the banking industry over the years since nationalization of Banks in 1969, particularly during the last decade (1990-2000). Having achieved the primary objectives of nationalization as envisaged by the Government policy framers at the time viz. a marked shift from class to mass banking, increasing the reach of the banking industry graphically through massive branch expansion, credit to the agriculture and rural sector and to function as an active arm of the Government for poverty alleviation, the most important issue before the industry at present is survival and growth in the vortex of strong cross currents that the economic liberalization has generated. The wide spread branch expansion programme resulted in a massive recruitment drive over the years for manning the operational units opened at the Government's directive. As a result the nationalized banking industry at present is characterized by a massive branch net-work and a bloated and highly unionized work force which combined with a low level of technology, has impaired the maneuverability of these organizations vis-a-vis the lean, compact, techno savvy, market driven and nimble footed new generation private banks which have come into the market over the last 9/10 years. These new entrants into the market are consistently chipping away at the market share of the nationalized banks especially in metro and urban centers thereby exposing the bottom line of the nationalized banks to severe strain.

It is now well understood that a healthy banking sector is the bedrock of a stable financial system. The renewed focus on the banking sector has been driven by two major considerations. Firstly, the growing universalisation and internationalization of banking operations have altered the face of banks from one of mere intermediator to one of provider of quick, efficient and consumer centric services. Secondly the widespread banking problems that have plagued large areas of the globe have raised a clutch of questions relating to linkages between banking reforms and reforms of other segments of the financial sector, exposure to sensitive sectors etc. It is therefore imperative especially in a developing economy like India where assets of the banking sector constitute a substantial proportion of financial sector assets, to promote robust financial practices and policies in respect of banks. In the wake of the recent financial crisis in different parts of the globe, there has been a renewed focus world wide on containing risks. The banking industry in India, in the new millennium, is also moving towards international best practices in banking supervision for achieving and maintaining stability and also to combat competition from global players effectively.

The Government, in recognition of the fact that the nationalized banking industry needs to augment their capital base to cope up with the changing operational environment, has permitted the banks to access the capital market both at home and abroad and has also permitted a reduction in the minimum Government shareholding in nationalized banks to 33 per cent. This landmark decision has wide ranging implications since the financial health of these banks would now be subjected to intense scrutiny of both the domestic and international rating agencies when the banks access the capital market for raising fresh funds to shore up their capital base.

Further, given the increasing internationalization of banking operation, Commercial Bank are often subject to significant mismatch between assets and liabilities with implication of several types of risk in view of which Assets Liability Management (ALM) Committees headed by top management functionaries have been set up. Moreover the increased complexity in banking operations and the need to prevent financial crisis of the type witnessed in South East Asia recently have necessitated up gradation of various risk management procedures and practices in the banking industry. A risk management system has therefore been put in place in the banks to enable them to take care of credit risk, interest rate risk, market risk and operational risk.

2.3 Major Reforms in the Indian Banking Sector

- Interest rate deregulation. Interest rates on deposits and lending have been deregulated with banks enjoying greater freedom to determine their rates.
- Adoption of prudential norms in terms of capital adequacy, asset
- Classification, income recognition, provisioning, exposure limits, investment fluctuation reserve, etc.
- Reduction in pre-emption – lowering of reserve requirements (SLR and CRR), thus releasing more lendable resources which banks can deploy profitably.
- Government equity in banks has been reduced and strong banks have been allowed to access the capital market for raising additional capital.
- Banks now enjoy greater operational freedom in terms of opening and swapping of branches, and banks with a good track record of profitability have greater flexibility in recruitment.
- New private sector banks have been set up and foreign banks permitted to expand their operations in India including through subsidiaries. Banks have also been allowed to set up
- Offshore Banking Units in Special Economic Zones.
- New areas have been opened up for bank financing: insurance, credit cards, infrastructure financing, leasing, gold banking, besides of course investment banking, asset management, factoring, etc.
- New instruments have been introduced for greater flexibility and better risk management: e.g. interest rate swaps, forward rate agreements, cross currency forward contracts, forward cover to hedge inflows under foreign direct investment, liquidity adjustment facility for meeting day-to-day liquidity mismatch.

- Several new institutions have been set up including the National Securities Depositories Ltd., Central Depositories Services Ltd., Clearing Corporation of India Ltd., Credit Information Bureau India Ltd.
- Limits for investment in overseas markets by banks, mutual funds and corporates have been liberalized. The overseas investment limit for corporates has been raised to 100 per cent of net worth and the ceiling of $100 million on prepayment of external commercial borrowings has been removed. MFs and corporates can now undertake FRAs with banks. Indians allowed maintaining resident foreign currency (domestic) accounts. Full convertibility for deposit schemes of NRIs introduced.
- Technology infrastructure for the payments and settlement system in the country has been strengthened with electronic funds transfer, Centralized Funds Management System, Structured Financial Messaging Solution, Negotiated Dealing System and move towards Real Time Gross Settlement.
- Adoption of global standards. Prudential norms for capital adequacy, asset classification, income recognition and provisioning are now close to global standards. RBI has introduced Risk Based Supervision of banks (against the traditional transaction based approach). Best international practices in accounting systems, corporate governance, payment and settlement systems, etc. are being adopted.
- Credit delivery mechanism has been reinforced to increase the flow of credit to priority sectors through focus on micro credit and Self Help Groups. The definition of priority sector has been widened to include food processing and cold storage, software up to Rs. 1 crore, housing above Rs. 10 lakh, selected lending through NBFCs, etc.
- RBI guidelines have been issued for putting in place risk management systems in banks. Risk Management Committees in banks address credit risk, market risk and operational risk. Banks have specialized committees to

measure and monitor various risks and have been upgrading their risk management skills and systems.

- The limit for foreign direct investment in private banks has been increased from 49 per cent to 74 per cent and the 10 per cent cap on voting rights has been removed. In addition, the limit for foreign institutional investment in private banks is 49 per cent.
- Wide ranging reforms have been carried out in the area of capital markets. Fresh investment in CPs, CDs are allowed only in dematerialized form. SEBI has reduced the settlement cycle from T+3 to T+2 from April 1, 2003 i.e. settlement of stock deals will be completed in two trading days after the trade is executed, taking the Indian stock trading system ahead of some of the developed equity markets. Stock exchanges will set up trade guarantee funds. Retail trading in Government securities has been introduced on NSE and BSE from January 16, 2003. A Serious Frauds Office is proposed to be set up. Fungibility of ADRs and GDRs allowed.
- Universal Banking has been introduced. With banks permitted to diversify into long-term finance and DFIs into working capital, guidelines have been put in place for the evolution of universal banks in an orderly fashion.

2.4 Universal Banking Defined

The Universal Bank emerged in Germany as a fruit of economic liberalism around the mid-19th century. It is defined as,

"A bank, usually a large one, which can offer a variety of services to its customers under one and the same roof."

(Perry, F.E. Dictionary of Banking, 1979)

Universal banking in general refers to the combination of commercial banking and investment banking. In a broader sense it encompasses financial services beyond commercial banking and investment banking, such as, insurance, leasing, investment advisory etc. However, universal banking does not mean that every institution conducts every type of business with every type of customer. In the spectrum of banking, specialized banking is on the one end and universal banking on the other.

Earlier financial institutions (FIs) used to cater to term loan requirements while commercial banks did working capital financing. Now, we have reached a stage where 'harmonisation' has taken place between the financial institutions and commercial banks, where they (the FIs) do working capital finance also and we do term loans also. In a limited sense that is universal banking. Further, it has evolved into a situation where we need to take care of the life cycle of the customer. Then, we have to have every product that he requires for his differing needs. So, when you have reached that stage when the bank is able to offer term loan, fixed assets loan, working capital finance, retail loans, etc., that makes a universe

Universal Banking includes not only services related to savings and loans but also investments. However in practice the term 'universal banks' refers to those banks that offer a wide range of financial services, beyond commercial banking and investment banking, insurance etc.

- Universal banking is a combination of commercial banking, investment banking and various other activities including insurance. If specialised banking is the one end universal banking is the other. This is most common in European countries.
- It results in greater economic efficiency in the form of lower cost, higher output and better products. However larger the banks, the greater the effects of their failure on the system. Also there is the fear that such institutions, by virtue of their sheer size, would gain monopoly power in the market, which can have significant undesirable consequences for economic efficiency. Also combining commercial and investment banking can gives rise to conflict of interests

2.5 Universal Banking in India

The Narsimham Committee II suggested that Development Financial Institutions (DFIs) should convert ultimately into either commercial banks or non-bank finance companies. The Khan Working Group held the view that DFIS should be allowed to become banks at the earliest. The RBI released a 'Discussion Paper' (DP) in January 1999 for wider public debate. The feedback on the discussion paper indicated that while the universal banking is desirable from the point of view of efficiency of resource use, there is need for caution in moving towards such a system by banks and DFIs. Major areas requiring attention are the status of financial sector reforms, the state of preparedness of the concerned institutions, the evolution of the regulatory regime and above all a viable transition path for institutions which are desirous of moving in the direction of universal banking. It is proposed to adopt the following broad approach for considering proposals in this area

The principle of "Universal Banking" is a desirable goal and some progress has already been made by permitting banks to diversify into investments and long-term financing and the DFIs to lend for working capital, etc. However, banks have certain special characteristics and as such any dilution of RBI's prudential and supervisory norms for conduct of banking business would be inadvisable. Further, any conglomerate in which a bank is present, should be subject to a consolidated approach to supervision and regulation.

Though the DFIs would continue to have a special role in the Indian financial System, until the debt market demonstrates substantial improvements in terms of liquidity and depth, any DFI, which wishes to do so, should have the option to transform into bank (which it can exercise), provided the prudential norms as applicable to banks are fully satisfied. To this end, a DFI would need to prepare a transition path in order to fully comply with the regulatory requirement of a bank. The DFI concerned may consult RBI for such transition arrangements. Reserve Bank will consider such requests on a case by case basis.

The regulatory framework of RBI in respect of DFIs would need to be strengthened if they are given greater access to short-term resources for meeting their financing requirements, which is necessary.

In due course, and in the light of evolution of the financial system, Narasimham Committee's recommendation that, ultimately there should be only banks and restructured NBFCs can be operationalised. In Indian context, the phenomenon of universal banking—as different from narrow banking—has been in the news in the recently. With the last Narasimham Committee and the Khan Committee reports recommending consolidation of the banking industry through mergers and integration of financial activities, the stage seems to be set for a debate on the entire issue. A universal bank is a 'one-stop' supplier for all financial products and activities, like deposits, short-term and long-term loans, insurance, investment banking etc. Global experience with universal banking has been varied. Universal banking has been prevalent in different forms in many European countries, such as Germany, Switzerland, France, Italy etc. For example, in these countries, commercial banks have been selling insurance products, which have been referred to as Banc assurance or Allfinanz.

After the stock market crash of 1929 and banking crisis of the 1930s, the US banned all forms of universal banking through what is known as the Glass- Steagall Act of 1933. This prohibited commercial banks from investment banking activities, taking equity positions in borrowing firms, selling insurance products etc. The idea was to mitigate risky behaviour by restricting commercial banks to their traditional activity of accepting deposits and lending.

Research on the effects of universal banking has been inconclusive as there is no clear-cut evidence in favour of or against it anywhere. Nevertheless, the United States has once again started moving cautiously towards universal banking through the Gramm-Leach-Bliley Act of 1999 which rolled back many of the earlier restrictions. Some recent phenomenon, like the merger between Citicorp (banking group) and Travelers (insurance group) confirmed the fact that universal banking is here to stay. Hence it becomes all the more imperative to know whether we need universal banks in India. And whether it is a more efficient concept than the traditional narrow banking? What are the benefits to banks from universal banking? The standard argument given everywhere—also by the various Reserve Bank committees and reports—in favour of universal banking is that it enables banks to exploit economies of scale and scope. What it means is that a bank can reduce average costs and thereby improve spreads if it expands its scale of operations and diversifies its activities.

2.6 Regulatory Issues for Conversion into a Universal Bank

1. **Reserve Requirements**: Compliance with the cash reserve ratio and statutory liquidity ratio requirements (under Section 42 of RBI Act, 1934, and Section 24 of the Banking Regulation Act, 1949, respectively) would be mandatory for an FI after its conversion into a universal bank.
2. **Permissible Activities:** Any activity of an FI currently undertaken but not permissible for a bank under Section 6(1) of the B.R. Act, 1949, may have to be stopped or divested after its conversion into a universal bank..
3. **Disposal of Non-banking Assets:** Any immovable property, howsoever acquired by an FI, would, after its conversion into a universal bank, be required to be disposed of within the maximum period of 7 years from the date of acquisition, in terms of Section 9 of the B.R. Act.
4. **Composition of the Board**: Changing the composition of the Board of Directors might become necessary for some of the FIs after their conversion into a universal bank, to ensure compliance with the provisions of Section 10(A) of the B.R. Act, which requires at least 51 per cent of the total number of directors to have special knowledge and experience.
5. **Prohibition on Floating Charge of Assets**: The floating charge, if created by an FI, over its assets, would require, after its conversion into a universal bank, ratification by the Reserve Bank of India under Section 14(A) of the B.R. Act,

since a banking company is not allowed to create a floating charge on the undertaking or any property of the company unless duly certified by RBI as required under the Section.

6. **Nature of Subsidiaries:** If any of the existing subsidiaries of an FI is engaged in an activity not permitted under Section 6(1) of the B.R Act, then on conversion of the FI into a universal bank, delinking of such subsidiary/activity from the operations of the universal bank would become necessary since Section 19 of the Act permits a bank to have subsidiaries only for one or more of the activities permitted under Section 6(1) of B.R. Act.
7. **Restriction on Investments:** An FI with equity investment in companies in excess of 30 per cent of the paid up share capital of that company or 30 per cent of its own paid-up share capital and reserves, whichever is less, on its conversion into a universal bank, would need to divest such excess holdings to secure compliance with the provisions of Section 19(2) of the B.R. Act, which prohibits a bank from holding shares in a company in excess of these limits.
8. **Connected Lending:** Section 20 of the B.R. Act prohibits grant of loans and advances by a bank on security of its own shares or grant of loans or advances on behalf of any of its directors or to any firm in which its director/manager or employee or guarantor is interested. The compliance with these provisions would be mandatory after conversion of an FI to a universal bank.
9. **Licensing**: An FI converting into a universal bank would be required to obtain a banking licence from RBI under Section 22 of the B.R. Act, for carrying on banking business in India, after complying with the applicable conditions.
10. **Branch Network**: An FI, after its conversion into a bank, would also be required to comply with extant branch licensing policy of RBI under which the new banks are required to allot at east 25 per cent of their total number of branches in semi-urban and rural areas.

11. **Assets in India**: An FI after its conversion into a universal bank, will be required to ensure that at the close of business on the last Friday of every quarter, its total assets held in India are not less than 75 per cent of its total demand and time liabilities in India, as required of a bank under Section 25 of the BR Act.
12. **Format of Annual Reports** : After converting into a universal bank, an FI will be required to publish its annual balance sheet and profit and loss account in the in the forms set out in the Third Schedule to the B.R Act, as prescribed for a banking company under Section 29 and Section 30 of the B.R Act.
13. **Managerial Remuneration of the Chief Executive Officers**: On conversion into a universal bank, the appointment and remuneration of the existing Chief Executive Officers may have to be reviewed with the approval of RBI in terms of the provisions of Section 35B of the B.R Act. The Section stipulates fixation of remuneration of the Chairman and Managing Director of a bank by Reserve Bank of India taking into account the profitability, net NPAs and other financial parameters. Under the Section, prior approval of RBI would also be required for appointment of Chairman and Managing Director.
14. **Deposit Insurance**: An FI, on conversion into a universal bank, would also be required to comply with the requirement of compulsory deposit insurance from DICGC up to a maximum of Rs. 1 lakh per account, as applicable to the banks.
15. **Authorized Dealer's License:** Some of the FIs at present hold restricted AD license from RBI, Exchange Control Department to enable them to undertake transactions necessary for or incidental to their prescribed functions. On conversion into a universal bank, the new bank would normally be eligible for full-fledged authorized dealer license and would also attract the full rigor of the Exchange Control Regulations applicable to the banks at present, including

prohibition on raising resources through external commercial borrowings.

16. **Priority Sector Lending**: On conversion of an FI to a universal bank, the obligation for lending to "priority sector" up to a prescribed percentage of their 'net bank credit' would also become applicable to it .
17. **Prudential Norms:** After conversion of an FI in to a bank, the extant prudential norms of RBI for the all-India financial institutions would no longer be applicable but the norms as applicable to banks would be attracted and will need to be fully complied with.

2.7 Advantages of Universal Banking

2.7.1 Multiple Utility of Activities: By diversifying, the bank can use its existing expertise in one type of financial service in providing the other types. So, it entails less cost in performing all the functions by one entity instead of separate specialized bodies. A bank possesses information on the risk characteristics of its clients, which it can use to pursue other activities with the same clients. This again saves cost compared to the case of different entities catering to the different needs of the same clients. A bank has an existing network of branches, which can act as shops for selling products like insurance. This way a big bank can reach the remotest client without having to take recourse to an agent. Many financial services are inter-linked activities, e.g. insurance and lending. A bank can use its instruments in one activity to exploit the other, e.g., in the case of project lending to the same firm which has purchased insurance from the bank.

2.7.2 Savings in Transaction Costs: Now, let us turn to the benefits accruing to the customers. The idea of 'one-stop-shopping' saves a lot of transaction costs and increases the speed of economic activity. Another manifestation of universal banking is a bank holding stakes in a firm. A bank's equity holding in a borrower firm acts as a signal for other investors on the health of the firm, since the lending bank is in a better position to monitor the firm's activities. This is useful from the investors' point of view.

2.7.3 Loss in Economies of Specialization: Then there is the problem of the bank indulging in too many risky activities. To account for this, appropriate regulation can be devised, which will ultimately benefit all the participants in the market, including the banks themselves. In spite of the associated problems, there seems to be a lot of interest expressed by banks and financial institutions in universal banking. In India, too, a lot of opportunities are there to be exploited. Banks, especially the financial institutions, are aware of it. And most of the groups have plans to diversify in a big way even though there might not be profits forthcoming in the short run due to the switching costs incurred in moving to a new business.

2.7.4 Lack of Expertise in Converting into Commercial Banks: Hitherto the business of the financial institutions has been confined to only `credit' with attendant forex business (with limitations). Apart from the proportion of existing NPAs in their balance sheets the FIs have to reckon with other important variables while moving towards commercial banking. Looking at the existing size of the financial institutions as compared to the bank with which merger is intended, the relatively short gestation period available to the bank to establish itself amidst the turbulent market/competition, the scenario is quite challenging. One might well ask what is the input from a financial institution in a merger to a relatively less asset-based bank? FIs have had a crucial role in the years following Independence: in the then prevalent conditions, financial institutions built up infrastructure contributed to a better industrial climate. The expertise in these fields may be sub served or enlarged appropriately. However is such expertise relevant for say small, retail loans-which are promising avenues for the banks of today?

2.7.5 Mismatch between Long and Short Term Business: Looked from another perspective, the financial institutions till yesterday are only for `long term' both on the assets and liabilities sides while commercial banks cater to `short term' businesses.

There was a marked demarcation, though not a `Chinese wall' between these two. With the advent of market economy, the gap is getting closed through `universal banking'. The subject is in the air for sometime but currently, rising NPAs and dearth of avenues for resources for the financial institutions in the wake of falling market sentiments in the recent period have accelerated the process. For a few of the FIs, survival itself might be at stake. On the risk parameters, the long term liabilities (at higher rates of interest, in the context of declining trends) will remain as they.

A re-look on the assets side strongly suggests that after netting the NPAs, the existing `mismatch' might well go up. Barring one or two of the new generation banks and foreign banks of course, the concept of ALM (asset-liability management) remains an academic subject. As far as the ICICI Bank is concerned, having only recently completed the takeover of Bank of Madura, it probably needs some more time to prepare for another drastic organizational upheaval.

2.7.6 Staff Incompatibility: It is pertinent to mention that amalgamation between banks in the past, from a personnel angle has not been at all compatible - the striking example of the New Bank of India with the Punjab National Bank is a case in point. But here, larger strength of non-bankers need to be groomed and accepted for banking counters! Dealings in financial institutions are structured in an easier convenient ``one to one basis" unlike in commercial banks where the personnel are rotated among different functions. There are sharp variations even in lending practices. For instance, in the FIs loan disbursals are structured over a period as compared to running accounts of borrowers in banks where they need to respond on the spot to the situations.

2.7.7 Compliance with BASEL II Norms: In the context of RBI's dictates, in conformity with Basle Committee prescriptions at the international level, to banks on `risk management', apparent risks in all spheres may call for special dispensations to the merged entity and thus one more class of banks (apart from public sector, old/new private sector, foreign banks) will emerge for the central bank to deal with. Lest unhealthy precedents are permitted, the central bank may have to envision a long term strategy to respond to emerging situations. In fact, RBI's policy to have permitted private banks to be established in the early Nineties has already been reviewed and yet another phase is now seen in regard to few banks which were then established. In fact, ever since RBI talked of `risk management' since 1998, except for some sporadic responses, it is yet to percolate at the top levels of management. So far it has been yet another jugglery with figures. One has to see the kind of disclosures in annual report of banks abroad on the risk parameters. The time is not far off for such compulsions from the international arenas (as the attraction for GAAP registration increases) to take hold. Failure or inaccuracies in disclosures may do greater harm at the national levels. For example, recently the regulatory authorities in the US demanded policy documents on certain aspects of banking business: here, practices exist sans any documents, notwithstanding the infamous securities scam of the 1990's; such permissiveness need to be contained. The RBI has on its record, such prescriptions but this need to be enforced with rigor to match the US practices.

2.8 Imperatives for Universal Banking

2.8.1 Improving Profitability: The most direct result of the above changes is increasing competition and narrowing of spreads and its impact on the profitability of banks. The challenge for banks is how to manage with thinning margins while at the same time working to improve productivity which remains low in relation to global standards. This is particularly important because with dilution in banks' equity, analysts and shareholders now closely track their performance. Thus, with falling spreads, rising provision for NPAs and falling interest rates, greater attention will need to be paid to reducing transaction costs. This will require tremendous efforts in the area of technology and for banks to build capabilities to handle much bigger volumes.

2.8.2 Reinforcing Technology: Technology has thus become a strategic and integral part of banking, driving banks to acquire and implement world class systems that enable them to provide products and services in large volumes at a competitive cost with better risk management practices. The pressure to undertake extensive computerization is very real as banks that adopt the latest in technology have an edge over others. Customers have become very demanding and banks have to deliver customized products through multiple channels, allowing customers access to the bank round the clock.

2.8.3 Risk Management: The deregulated environment brings in its wake risks along with profitable opportunities, and technology plays a crucial role in managing these risks. In addition to being exposed to credit risk, market risk and operational risk, the business of banks would be susceptible to country risk, which will be heightened as controls on the movement of capital are eased. In this context, banks are upgrading their credit assessment and risk management skills and retraining staff, developing a cadre of specialists and introducing technology driven management information systems.

2.8.4 Sharpening Skills: The far-reaching changes in the banking and financial sector entail a fundamental shift in the set of skills required in banking. To meet increased competition and manage risks, the demand for specialized banking functions, using IT as a competitive tool is set to go up. Special skills in retail banking, treasury, risk management, foreign exchange, development banking, etc., will need to be carefully nurtured and built. Thus, the twin pillars of the banking sector i.e. human resources and IT will have to be strengthened.

2.8.5 Greater Customer Orientation: In today's competitive environment, banks will have to strive to attract and retain customers by introducing innovative products, enhancing the quality of customer service and marketing a variety of products through diverse channels targeted at specific customer groups.

2.8.6 Corporate Governance: Besides using their strengths and strategic initiatives for creating shareholder value, banks have to be conscious of their responsibilities towards corporate governance. Following financial liberalization, as the ownership of banks gets broad based the importance of institutional and individual shareholders will increase. In such a scenario, banks will need to put in place a code for corporate governance for benefiting all stakeholders of a corporate entity.

2.8.7 International Standards: Introducing internationally followed best practices and observing universally acceptable standards and codes is necessary for strengthening the domestic financial architecture. This includes best practices in the area of corporate governance along with full transparency in disclosures. In today's globalised world, focusing on the observance of standards will help smooth integration with world financial markets.

2.9 Universal Banking: Implications

Universal banking has a wide spectrum of implications.

2.9.1 Portfolio Risk: Permitting banks to acquire more substantial equity holdings than they can now could diminish the risk taken by banks or increase it. Economists and regulators have long understood that the riskiness of returns on common stock exceeds that of debt, other things being equal. For many years, a principal reason for separating banking from commerce has been the belief that some activities, including equity and real estate investment, were too risky. It is now well understood that risk can be reduced by diversification. Equity and other types of assets might, in themselves, be relatively risky, but if they have a diversifying effect on other investments, they can reduce risk in a portfolio of assets by smoothing revenue streams over time. So, for example, a banking conglomerate that included an automobile manufacturer might find that, although interest rate increases during an expansion reduced revenues from financial services, the reduced revenues were offset by increased revenues from automobile sales.

Alternatively, in a steep recession, with revenues from automobile sales declining, the offset might come from favorable interest rate spreads on financial services. According to empirical evidence, diversifying by combining banking and commerce may reduce risk. The potential, however, is likely to differ among banks of different size. So, for example, the potential gain for large banking organizations with international operations that already permit equity investments is unlikely to be as great as for smaller regional and local banks whose current investments opportunities are more limited. Moreover, whether or not a banking organization actually chooses to diversify will depend on more factors than the scope of permitted activities. There is also evidence indicating that widening the scope of permitted activities through holding companies has increased the volatility of bank returns.

2.9.2 Economies of Scale: Eliminating barriers between banking and commerce could conceivably yield economies of scale and/or scope. Economies of scale are manifest in lower average costs when the scale of production of a specified product increases. Economies of scope lower average costs when different products within one organization share inputs. Realization of such economies for a wide range of banking services would, under competitive conditions, reduce prices paid by bank customers. Combining banking with commercial firms makes bigger organizations. Big diversified organizations could increase scale if some of the products of the combining firms were enough alike to use the same production process, e.g. a bank's automobile financing and an automobile company's automobile financing. Liberalization of branch banking restrictions in recent years has facilitated large scale without the involvement of commercial firms. By acquiring a small bank, a large bank can reduce the other's high average costs.

2.9.3 Conflict of Interests: The possibility for multiple conflicts of interest when a bank is an owner of the company to whom it is lending, or whose securities it is underwriting, raise issues that have a long history. Among other things, the creditor-underwriter-owner combination also raises questions about the availability and use of insider information. Potential conflicts that have been cited from time to time include the following:

1. A bank may extend credit to a company in which it has an ownership interest, independent of the company's

creditworthiness, to assist the company and increase the value of its stock. Such an extension would conflict with the interest of its depositors, its safety and soundness, and the integrity of the deposit insurance fund. Further, rival companies, unaffiliated with the banking organization, might be subjected to unfair credit terms.

2. If bank managers own, in their own right, equity in the same commercial company that the bank controls, managers would have an incentive, independent of the interests of the bank's stockholders, to increase the value of the company, possibly at the expense of the bank. The conflict, in this case, is between the interests of bank management and the bank's stockholders.
3. Similarly a bank may purchase the debt or equity securities of a company that it owns and to whom it is a creditor to temporarily increase the value of a company's stock and, in the extreme, provide it with funds to repay its bank loans. Such transactions would also conflict with the interests of depositors, safety and soundness, and the integrity of the deposit insurance fund.
4. A bank may come to the rescue of a failing company by moving bad assets from its subsidiary or affiliate to the bank. It may or may not be a rational shift aimed at protecting the banking organization's reputation and future profitability. The potential conflict in this case is between the interests of the bank's stockholders, on the one hand, and the interests of its creditors, bank supervision, the deposit insurance fund, and taxpayers on the other.
5. A bank may obtain substantial amounts of inside information that it might act on in its security dealing. If the information is withheld from its securities customers, the bank could benefit at their expense. In the extreme, the bank may use inside information to sell weak securities from its own portfolio to its customers, either directly or through a managed investment fund, and to purchase strong securities in advance of publicly available information.

The conflict between its own interests and the interests of its securities customers may be exacerbated by a conflict, under current law, between the requirement that it not reveal or act on inside information and the obligation of a dealer to provide all relevant information to its customers. Conflicts may be exacerbated by the organizational form. In either an affiliate or subsidiary structure, ownership and creditor relationships between a bank, its officials, and the subsidiaries or affiliates are likely to be important. Universal banks, in which all activities are conducted within the bank itself or in subsidiaries or affiliates that are owned pro rata by the organization's stockholders, carry the least danger of creating incentives that exacerbate potential conflicts.

2.9.4 Global Competition and Bank Viability: If narrowing or eliminating the separation between banking and commerce reduces risk, moderates the asymmetric information problem, and, for these and other reasons, lowers average costs, foreign banks with broader powers should have an advantage in competition with local banks. If nothing more, foreign banks should have an advantage in maintaining loan customers in whom they have an ownership interest.

2.9.5 Financial Markets: On banking developments in other countries, comparisons suggest that financial markets are less developed in countries in which banks have played a larger role in providing equity and long-term credit as well as short-term credit. It has frequently been suggested that because many transactions in Germany were executed through banks rather than through markets, universal banking has been at least partly responsible for Germany's weak capital markets. In the mid-1980s, one study of capital markets in Germany reported signs of "fragmentation." The size of issues was small, turnover was relatively low, the market was shallow, and the market's formal operations were limited. The German banks' role as "an all purpose financial institution, the absence of large non-bank financial institutions, the banks' freedom to invest in equities and the German tax system," it concluded, "may all contribute to the country's narrow capital market development."

2.9.6 Production Sector: Prospective banking/commerce changes may directly affect not only the financial sector but also the commercial or production sector of the economy. Potential impacts can be considered in a number of areas, including economic growth and stability, competition, concentration, and small business lending. There are, moreover, a variety of other allocational efficiency considerations that also merit attention.

2.9.7 Economic Growth and Stability: The relative contributions of banking-commerce relationships to economic growth and stability have been a focal point of comparison between Germany and United States. The cost of capital to commercial firms, the pace of innovation and technological change, and susceptibility of the different economies to systemic events all has potentially differential effects on economic growth and stability.

2.9.8 Technological Change and Innovation: Technological improvements and innovation accounts, through improved productivity, for a substantial share of economic growth in the economy. It is conceivable that larger and better diversified banks would contribute to more rapid technological innovation. Large companies have an advantage in supporting research and innovation; diversification might contribute because of the "cross fertilization" of ideas and the cross-selling of new products, among other things. How important size and diversification are, however, is unclear, given the possibilities for sluggishness in large, complex organizations and the seeming willingness of small and new businesses to take greater risks. The combination of banking with commercial firms will result in larger and more diversified organizations. Improved efficiency and lower costs of capital, if they materialized, might better support innovation both in banking and in industry. There has, however, been little or no investigation into the effects of bank size and diversification on innovation. In other areas, empirical studies have not provided consistent results.

2.9.9 Systemic Risk: Concern about systemic risk transcends the financial and commercial sectors. To the extent a systemic event develops in any sector, it is likely to affect the entire economy. The ability of banking organizations to diversify could provide some protection against distress that might otherwise lead to systemic problems. Whatever the extent of geographic and/or product diversification, systemic problems may still occur, for example, from oil crises, stock market crashes, and real estate busts; that is, from the kind of risk that cannot be reduced by diversification. The timing and specific nature of such shocks are not predictable. Less bank aversion to risk at the end of a long expansion has been identified as a contributing cause of systemic problems.119 objectively, shocks become increasingly likely with the lengthening of an economic expansion in which optimism flourishes.

2.9.10 Risk-sharing and Inter-temporal Smoothing: The existence of systemic risk raises the issue of risk-sharing. It is a well-established principal of modern financial analysis that well-functioning financial markets permit portfolio diversification and reduction or elimination of the risk associated with variability in the return to individual securities. Further, financial markets permit the adjustment of portfolio risk in accordance with preferences, as well as the hedging of risks. Diversification, portfolio adjustment, and hedging involve the exchange of risk among market participants. They can be termed "cross-sectional risk-sharing," since "different individuals are exchanging risks at a given point in time."

On the other hand, there are important kinds of risk that, as a practical matter, cannot in general be diversified or hedged. These include risks that arise out of shocks that affect the entire economy, such as the oil crisis of the early 1970s and the sudden and substantial upward movement in interest rates in the early 1980s. These kinds of risk can be reduced, however, through institutional mechanisms that stabilize investors' income streams over time. Such mechanisms also involve risk-sharing that can be termed "inter-temporal smoothing."

2.9.11 Competition and Concentration: How combining banking and commerce would affect competition and concentration are longstanding concerns. A traditional criticism of universal banking in Germany and the close association between banks and commercial firms in Japan has been that small and new businesses are discriminated against in obtaining credit. This same criticism has periodically been made against large banks in the United States. A fundamental problem in evaluating such criticisms is that it is difficult to differentiate between the effects of business size and credit risk on differential rates, terms, and credit availability. Even though combining banking and commerce, coupled with continuing mergers, will result in larger banking organizations, no issue need arise as long as adequate sources of credit remain for small businesses. However, small businesses are typically more dependent on bank credit than large, and it is possible that the shifts now occurring will diminish the availability of credit to them.

2.9.12 Industrial Policy: Germany and Japan have, in the past, directed equity investments by banks to meet government objectives for industrialization and military preparation. Banks have been elements in their industrial policy. Banks have also been used to meet public objectives. Comparative experience suggests that universal banking is a useful mechanism for industrial policy. While economic analysis strongly supports some government direction of resources, there have been in the United States, particularly during recessions, debates on whether government should identify and support key industries to enable them to compete in world markets. The integration of banking and commerce would not in itself resolve this debate, but it would create a convenient mechanism for such support.

2.9.13 Corporate Governance: A universal banking system's asymmetric information/transaction costs and competitive imperfections may cause real resources to be allocated less efficiently. Corporate governance in a universal banking system can affect resource allocation for good or bad. Characteristic of universal systems has been that banks rather than the markets determine resource allocation. So, for example, if RBI eased monetary policy, it might confront the complaint that it was doing so for the benefit of large commercial firms affiliated with large commercial banks. In times of stress, transfers of credit to commercial company affiliates or subsidiaries may be difficult to control.

2.9.14 Organizational Structure: The principal aim is to protect the bank from the risks involved in commercial activities and to prevent the transmission of whatever subsidy might exist for the bank to non-banking activities. Firewalls are intended to bolster corporate separateness. The assumption is that firewalls are more effective between separate corporations than within a corporation (e.g., between a bank and its trust department).

2.9.15 Large and Complex Size: As banking organizations grow larger and more complex, financial markets and bank managers are likely to perceive some as being too big to fail. Such perception creates bank incentives to take excessive risk (moral hazard). Supervisors of banking organizations perceived as too big to fail are likely to depend heavily on risk-adjusted capital requirements for the bank (if not the banking organization), risk-adjusted deposit insurance premiums, and intensive supervision. From a competitive perspective, too big to fail provides advantages to large banking organizations relative to small ones. Unless market perceptions are built on a clear understanding that banks, but not their subsidiaries and affiliates, are supportable, and that strict enforcement of firewalls will be maintained, the "corporate veil" would not be adequate to prevent the transmission of too-big-to- fail advantages to commercial firms through lower organizational costs of capital.

2.9.16 Extension of Banking Regulation: Combining banking with commercial activities would at least require this multitude to work in a more coordinated fashion. Banks would likely enter businesses that are regulated by other types of agencies. Banks might own or be owned by public utilities such as telephone companies, transportation companies, oil/gas pipelines, and power companies. Expansion through separate subsidiaries or affiliates may bring so-called functional regulation the regulatory supervision of a complex company by many agencies according to their expertise. Whether or not that happens, the continued existence of firewalls and any continuation of cross-guarantees call for close cooperation among the several bank regulators. If combined banking-commercial organizations measure and manage their risk on a consolidated basis, another important reason exists for such cooperation. If new banking-commercial combinations involve new interfaces between banking and non-banking regulatory agencies, issues regarding the efficacy of the current regulatory structure, similar to those that have arisen in debates on bank expansion into securities and insurance, are likely to develop.

2.9.17 Socio-political and Cultural Issues: In considering socio-political and cultural issues, definitions are useful. Political systems include the relationships between people and their political leaders, methods of choosing political leaders, and factors affecting political decisions. Social systems include group structure in society, relationships among groups, and the duration of such groups. Both political and social systems may be subsumed under the amorphous term "culture." Cultural characteristics include perceptions of and attitudes toward some of which have been to Comparison with the United States suggests that these issues are not unique to universal banking. But there is a difference in degree. The prospect exists that the large banking-commerce conglomerates will have an increased influence on public policy by virtue of their size and importance. Perceptive analysis of the past half-century has found a close relationship between political democracy and a free market system. In the United States, markets have grown with little government interference and abundant opportunity for small and new business; the financial and economic system in the United States has also been compatible with political democracy.

The long-run prospects, however, are very encouraging. At present, only an 'arms-length' relationship between a bank and an insurance entity has been allowed by the regulatory authority, i.e.

the Insurance Regulatory and Development Authority (IRDA). This means that commercial banks can enter insurance business either by acting as agents or by setting up joint ventures with insurance companies. And the RBI allows banks to only marginally invest in equity (5 per cent of their outstanding credit).

2.10 Conclusion

The face of banking is changing rapidly. Competition is going to be tough and with financial liberalisation under the WTO, banks in India will have to benchmark themselves against the best in the world. For a strong and resilient banking and financial system, therefore, banks need to go beyond peripheral issues and tackle significant issues like improvements in profitability, efficiency and technology, while achieving economies of scale through consolidation and exploring available cost-effective solutions. Universal banking is evolving and numerous examples such as Citigroup, ICICI Bank and HDFC Bank are rapidly moving to integrate and automate their diverse operations and processes. Automation of end-to-end business processes was outlined as the key driver for the growth of major financial markets globally; automation is also the key driver for all major initiatives such as Straight through Processing (STP) and the integration of various exchanges, and settlement and clearing organizations. Development financial institutions (DFIs) can turn themselves into banks, but have to adhere to the statutory liquidity ratio and cash reserve requirements meant for banks. Even then, some groups like the HDFC (commercial banking and insurance joint venture with Standard Assurance), ICICI (commercial banking), SBI (investment banking) etc., have already started diversifying from their traditional activities through setting up subsidiaries and joint ventures. In a recent move, the Life Insurance Corporation increased its stakes in Corporation Bank and is planning to sell insurance to the customers of the Bank. Corporation Bank itself has been planning to set up an insurance subsidiary since a long time. Even a specialized DFI, like IIBI, is now talking of turning into a universal bank. All these can be seen as steps towards an ultimate culmination of financial intermediation in India into universal banking.

References

Age of Universal Banking. African Business, June 2001 Issue 266, p. 22.

Are German-type Universal Banks Superior in Performance to other Types of Universal Banks? By: Wonsik Sul; Joon Seok Oh. Journal of Financial Management & Analysis, Jul-Dec. 99, Vol. 12 Issue 2, p. 18.

Conflict of Interest in Universal Banking: Bank Lending, Stock Underwriting, and Fund Management. By Ber, Hedva; Yafeh, Yishay; Yosha, Oved. Journal of Monetary Economics, Feb. 2001, Vol. 47 Issue 1, pp. 189-218.

Consolidation and Universal Banking. By Saunders, Anthony. *Journal of Banking* & Finance, Feb. 99, Vol. 23 Issue 2-4, pp. 693-695.

Expansion of Commercial Banking Powers ... or, Universal Banking is the Cart, not the Horse. By: Boyd, John H. Journal of *Banking &* Finance, Feb99, Vol. 23 Issue 2-4, p. 655-662.

Experts Split on Safety of Universal Banks. By: Seiberg, Jaret. American Banker, 11/14/97, Vol. 162 Issue 220, p. 2.

The European Influence. By: Stein, Robert W. Best's Review, Oct2000, Vol. 101 Issue 6, p. 165.

The Future of Universal Banking. By: Rich, Georg; Walter, Christian. CATO Journal, Fall 93, Vol. 13 Issue 2, p. 289.

Universal Banking and US Banking in the 1990s. By: Cameron, Colleen W.. International Journal of Social Economics, 1995, Vol. 22 Issue 4, p. 12.

Universal Banking is Government's Aim. Emerging European Markets, Oct97, Vol. 1 Issue 2, p. 4.

Universal Banking By: Benston, George J. Journal of Economic Perspectives, Summer 94, Vol. 8 Issue 3, pp. 121-143.

Universal Banking: A Shareholder Value Perspective. By: Walter, Ingo. European Management Journal, Aug. 97, Vol. 15 Issue 4, p. 344.

3

Role of Information Technology in Banking Sector

Puja Arora, Deepak Kumar and Monika Kansal

Information technology refers to the acquisition, processing, storage and dissemination of all types of information using computer technology and telecommunication systems. Technology includes all maters concerned with the furtherance of computer science and technology and with the design, development, installation and implementation of information system and applications. Information technology architecture is an integrated framework for acquiring and evolving IT to achieve strategic goals. It has both logical and technical components. Computer hardware and software, voice, data, network, satellite, other telecommunications technologies, multimedia are application development tools. These technologies are used for the input, storage, processing and communication of information.

Information technology includes ancillary equipment, software, firmware and similar procedures, services etc. Modern high throughput technologies are providing vast amounts of the sequences, expressions and functional data for genes and protein. One of the most difficult challenges is turning this enormous pool of information into useful scientific insight and novel therapeutic products.

3.1 Introduction

With the globalization trends world over it is difficult for any nation big or small, developed or developing, to remain isolated from what is happening around. For a country like India, which is one of the most promising emerging markets, such isolation is nearly impossible. More particularly in the area of Information technology, where India has definitely an edge over its competitors, remaining away or uniformity of the world trends is untenable. Financial sector in general and banking industry in particular is the largest spender and beneficiary from information technology. This endeavors to relate the international trends in it with the Indian banking industry.

The last lot includes possibly all foreign banks and newly established Private sector banks, which have fully computerized all the operations. With these variations in the level of information technology in Indian banks, it is useful to take account of the trends in information technology internationally as also to see the comparative position with Indian banks. The present article starts with the banks perception when they get into IT up gradation. All the trends in IT sector are then discussed to see their relevance to the status of Indian banks.

3.2 IT Considerations

Since the early nineties, each Indian bank has done some IT improvement effort. The first and foremost compulsion is the fierce competition. While deciding on the required architecture for the IT consideration is given to following realities.

- **Meeting Internal Requirement:** The requirements of the banks are different individually depending upon their nature and volume of business; focus on a particular segment, spread of branches and a like. Many a times banks do have the required information but it is scattered. The operating units seldom know the purpose of gathering the information by their higher authorities.
- **Effective in Data Handling:** As stated earlier the banks have most of the needed data but are distributed. Further the cost of collection of data and putting the same to use is prohibitively high. The accuracy and timeliness of data generation becomes the causalities in the process. Best of the intentions on computerization are wished away because there is non-visible reduction in cost/efforts/time required for the required data gathering.

- **Extending Customer Services:** Addressing to rising customers expectations is significant particularly in the background of increased competition. In case bank A is unable to provide the required service at a competitive price and in an accurate manner with speed. There is always a bank IT at its next-door waiting to hire the customer. Awareness of customers about the availability of services and their pricing as also available options have brought into sharp focus the issue of customer satisfaction.
- **Creative Support for New Product Development:** It has become necessary for the banks to vitalize the process of product development. Marketing functionaries needs a lot of information not only from the outside sources but also from within the banks. Banks are looking to retail segment as the future market places for sales efforts. Having full-fledged information of existing customer is the key for this purpose. The emergences of data requirement and an appropriate architecture to support the same are significant issues to be handled in this regard.
- **End-user Development of the Non-technical Staff:** Banking being a service industry, it is the staff at counters that delivers the products. In Indian scenario, virtual banking is likely to have a few more years to establish. The dependence on counter staff is unavoidable. The staff is large in number and the majority is non-technical. The customer satisfaction levels at the counter determine the ultimate benefit of IT offensive. Giving due consideration to this aspect in choosing architecture is necessary.

3.3 Trends in Information Technology

Certain trends have been visualized of information technology in banking sector all over the world.

3.3.1 Outsourcing: Outsourcing is one of the most talked about as also a controversial issue. The drivers for getting in to outsourcing are many to include gaps in IT expectations and the reality, demystification of computerization in general and IT in particulars, trend towards focusing on core competencies, increased legitimacy of outsourcing and intention of getting out of worries and sort of up gradation of hardware and software versions. Not that the practice is new as earlier it was refused to as 'buying time' or 'service bureau'. What is needed is the clear of outsourcing, beside a definite plan to be more competitive after outsourcing. It is necessary to have checks an balances to monitor vendor performance. Cost aspects merit consideration, as also a decision on the part of the process to be outsourced shall be significance. Exit route and resource on the amount of failure after outsourcing are the other issue to be looked onto. Not withstanding these risks, outsourcing has come to stay.

3.3.2 Integration: One of the IT trend is moving from hierarchy to team approach. The purpose is to see an alternative to retooling, to react speedily and to develop capabilities rather than exploiting them. Such integration is necessary so as to address to prevalent situations:

- Functions needing data and not getting from others.
- Sending data to those who do not want to require them.
- Global data exist but do not travel to required business functions

Indian banks seem to follow this trend through the sincere re-design as described earlier. Instead of vertically divided pyramid type organizational set-ups, banks are now being to have separate group like finance, international consumer banking, industrial/commercial credit and alike

3.3.3 From Solo to Partnership: With the development of IT, two things are taking place simultaneously. The work force as a percentage of total staff is going down and spending on IT as percentage of total spending is going up. The forms of partnership can include binding by superior service, accommodation in service sharing network, equal partnership and situations, where survival is threatened. At times, the partnership becomes necessary to get out of areas where there is no competitive advantage. Low development cost or wider geographical coverage is the aspects that create such partnership. Instances are not frequent, where joint ventures have been found with the IT vendors.

3.3.4 Distinctive Edge: It is always said that many use but a few make use of IT. Historically, the emphasis is on using IT for large volumes like payrolls, balancing the books, the consolidation etc. That realization on having IT as matter of competitive edge has come about very lately. It is recognized that customer service is not an easy thing to provide, but IT is used as a mean. It does give value additions and erases barriers for competitors to enter. Banks understand that the cost of cultivating the new customer is 5 to 6 times of retaining the old one. Customer normally switches banks due to poor service. The appreciation of these facts has compelled the banks world over to look upon IT as a instrument to create distinctive edge over competitors. The private sector banks that were established in 1990's as a part of finance sector reforms did make good of IT to have an edge over the others. The foreign banks operating in India have also been able to market IT superiority as a distinctive edge. The public sector banks are still to make use of IT in this regard, although they are blessed with huge information base all across the country. While steps are mooted in this direction by leading public sector banks, more offensive postures are necessary.

3.3.5 IT as Profit Centre: In the embryonic phases, IT was looked upon a means to get rid of high processing cost and time and to convert the manual operation with high volume/low complexity in two mechanical ones. With the evolutionary the process, it was seen as the best means of generating, MIS. The same approach gave the status of DSS to IT. All along, IT has been recognized as the service function in Indian Banks. However, the new trend that is emerging is considering IT as a profit center. The cost benefits analysis of having IT or otherwise is one part. But having IT set up to generate income for the organization is the new beginning. Getting jobs from outside the bank for processing data and the like are the current trends. The outsourcing done by others is the business, cater to by these organizations the trend of this kind is not deserved in Indian situation particularly banks. The Banks have been able to just manage what is to consider as their responsibility as IT, within the individual banks.

3.3.6 Prospering in Down Market: The trend suggests that when there is adown turn in the market place, Pro-active corporations take the benefit of available unutilized resources to upgrade and revisit technology issues. This is seen as the right time to establish the R & D center for IT. There are false notions about technology and its capability. Some misconceptions include:

- Best-fit possible technology is implemented.
- System solution is good enough and there is need to look into user expectations.
- Innovations are generally successful.
- Success is related only to novel ideas.
- Technology is the sole determinant of business success, and
- Measures and standards i.e. audit and inspection issues stand in the way of innovation.

The time available to debate on similar issues is ample and these false notions get clarified during the down market. Eventually, the decision makers reach a consensus that IT is not a panacea but it is an enabler that too when well supported by BRP (Business Process Re-engineering), human resources initiatives, physical infrastructure and responsive organization set up.

3.3.7 Leading to Downsizing: The IT initiative is making the organization lean and flat. For IT functionaries downsizing means transferring computing power from mainframe to the personal computer and workstations. Downsizing is a typical issue faced with associated problems. Absence of top management commitment, lack of understanding of the prevalent IT infrastructure, doing too much and too fast and undertaking the exercise without a framework for controlling the downsizing operations are primarily the situations that create adversities in downsizing. In any case the trend of downsizing is very much existent in the IT environment.

3.3.8 Getting Competitive Intelligence: IT is now seen as a resource for gathering and dissemination of executive information system (EIS). The purpose is to minimize that the bombarding and focusing on the relevance, accuracy and timeliness of the information particularly about the competitors such information enhances follow up and tracks early warning on competitor move and also customer expectations.

As far as Indian banks are concerned individually, they have to compete with other banking industry participants as also with other players in the financial sector. The competition from for insurance and government notes and saving, mutual funds and the like is always forthcoming particularly because of attendant tax benefits. Collection of required information and using the same for business purpose is constrained by the availability of the information, its volume and diversity. As such it may take some time for this trend to be visible in Indian banking scenario.

3.4 Recent Developments in Banking Sector

3.4.1 Internet: Internet is a networking of computers. In this marketing message can be transferred and received worldwide. The data can be sent and received in any part of the world. In no time, Internet facility can do many a job for us. It includes the following:

- This net can work as electronic mailing system.
- It can have access to the distant database, which may be a newspaper of foreign country.
- We can exchange our ideas through Internet. We can make contact with anyone who is a linked with Internet.
- On Internet, we can exchange letters, figures/diagrams and music recording.

Internet is a fast developing net and is of utmost important for public sector undertaking, Education Institutions, Research Organization etc.

3.4.2 Society for Worldwide Inter-bank Financial Telecommunications (SWIFT): SWIFT, as a co- operative society was formed in May 1973 with 239 participating banks from 15 countries with its headquarters at Brussels. It started functioning in May 1977. Reserve Bank of India and 27 other public sector banks as well as 8 foreign banks in India have obtained the membership of the SWIFT. SWIFT provides have rapid, secure, reliable and cost effective mode of transmitting the financial messages worldwide. At present more than 3000 banks are the members of the network. To cater to the growth in messages, SWIFT was upgrade in the 80s and this version is called SWIFT–II. Banks in India are hooked to SWIFT–II system.

SWIFT is a method of the sophisticated message transmission of international repute. This is highly cost effective, reliable and safe means of fund transfer.

- This network also facilitates the transfer of messages relating to fixed deposit, interest payment, debit-credit statements, foreign exchange etc.
- This service is available throughout the year, 24 hours a day.
- This system ensure against any loss of mutilation against transmission.
- It serves almost all financial institution and selected range of other users.

It is clear from the above benefit of SWIFT that it is very beneficial in effective customer service. SWIFT has extended its range to users like brokers, trust and other agents.

3.4.3 Automated Teller Machine (ATM): ATM is an electronic machine, which is operated by the customer himself to make deposits, withdrawals and other financial transactions. ATM is a step in improvement inn customer service. ATM facility is available to the customer 24 hours a day.

The customer is issued an ATM card. This is a plastic card, which bears the customer's name. This card is magnetically coded and can be read by this machine. Each cardholder is provided with a secret personal Identification Number (PIN). When the customer wants to use the card, he has to insert his plastic card in the slot of the machine. After the card is a recognized by the machine, the customer enters his personal identification number. After establishing the authentication of the customers, the ATM allows the customer to enter the amount to be withdrawn by him. After processing that transaction and finding sufficient balances in his account, the output slot of ATM give the required cash to him. When the transaction is completed, the ATM ejects the customer's card.

3.4.4 Cash Dispensers: Cash withdrawal is the basic service rendered by the bank branches. The cash payment is made by the cashier or teller of the cash dispenses is an alternate to time saving. The operations by this machine are cheaper than manual operations and this machine is cheaper and fast than that of ATM. The customer is provided with a plastic card, which is magnetically coated. After completing the formalities, the machine allows the machine the transactions for required amount.

3.4.5 Electronic Clearing Service: In 1994, RBI appointed a committee to review the mechanization in the banks and also to review the electronic clearing service. The committee recommended in its report that electronic clearing service-credit clearing facility should be made available to all corporate bodies/Government institutions for making repetitive low value payment like dividend, interest, refund, salary, pension or commission, it was also recommended by the committee Electronic Clearing Service – Debit clearing may be introduced for pre-authorized debits for payments of utility bills, insurance premium and installments to leasing and financing companies. RBI has been necessary step to introduce these schemes, Initially in Chennai, Mumbai, Calcutta and New Delhi.

3.4.6 Banknet: Banknet is a first national level network in India, which was commissioned in February 1991. It is communication network established by RBI on the basis of recommendation of the committee appointed by it under the chairmanship of the executive director T.N.A. Lyre. Banknet has two phases: Banknet–I and Banknet–II.

Areas of Operation and Application of Banknet:

- The message of banking transaction can be transferred in the form of codes from the city to the other.
- Quick settlement of transactions and advices.

- Improvement in customer service – withdrawal of funds is possible from any member branch.
- Easy transfer of data and other statements to RBI.
- Useful in foreign exchange dealings.
- Access to SWIFT through Banknet is easily possible.

3.4.7 Chip Card: The customer of the bank is provided with a special type of credit card which bears customer's name, code etc. The credit amount of the customer account is written on the card with magnetic methods. The computer can read these magnetic spots. When the customer uses this card, the credit amount written on the card starts decreasing. After use of number of times, at one stage, the balance becomes nil on the card. At that juncture, the card is of no use. The customer has to deposit cash in his account for re– use of the card. Again the credit amount is written on the card by magnetic means.

3.4.8 Phone Banking: Customers can now dial up the bank's designed telephone number and he by dialing his ID number will be able to get connectivity to bank's designated computer. The software provided in the machine interactive with the computer asking him to dial the code number of the service required by him and suitably answers him. By using Automatic voice recorder (AVR) for simple queries and transactions and manned phone terminals for complicated queries and transactions, the customer can actually do entire non-cash relating banking on telephone: Anywhere, Anytime.

3.4.9 Tele-banking: Tele banking is another innovation, which provided the facility of 24 hour banking to the customer. Tele-banking is based on the voice processing facility available on bank computers. The caller usually a customer calls the bank anytime and can enquire balance in his account or other transaction history. In this system, the computers at bank are connected to a telephone link with the help of a modem. Voice processing facility is provided in the software. This software identifies the voice of caller and provides him suitable reply. Some banks also use telephonic answering machine but this is limited to some brief functions. This is only telephone answering system and now tele-banking. Tele banking is becoming popular since queries at ATM's are now becoming too long.

3.4.10 Internet Banking: Internet banking enables a customer to do banking transactions through the bank's website on the Internet. It is a system of accessing accounts and general information on bank products and services through a computer while sitting in its office or home. This is also called virtual banking. It is more or less bringing the bank to you computer. In traditional banking one has to approach the branch in person, to withdraw cash or deposit a cheque or request a statement of accounts etc. but Internet banking has changed the way of banking. Now one can operate all these types of transaction on his computer through website of bank. All such transactions are encrypted; using sophisticated multi-layered security architecture, including firewalls and filters. One can be rest assured that one's transactions are secure and confidential.

3.4.11 Mobile Banking: Mobile banking facility is an extension of internet banking. The bank in association with the cellular service providers offers this service. For this service, mobile phone should either be SMS or WAP enabled. These facilities are available even to those customers with only credit card accounts with the bank.

3.4.12 Any where Banking: With expansion of technology, it is now possible to obtain financial details from the bank from remote locations. Basic transaction can be effected from far away places. Automated Teller Machines are playing an important role in providing remote services to the customers. Withdrawals from other stations have been possible due to inter-station connectivity of ATM's. The Rangarajan committee had also suggested the installation of ATM at non-branch locations, airports, hotels, Railway stations, Office Computers, Remote Banking is being further extended to the customer's office and home.

3.4.13 Voice Mail: Talking of answering systems, there are several banks mainly foreign banks now offering very advanced touch tone telephone answering service which route the customer call directly to the department concerned and allow the customer to leave a message for the concerned desk or department, if the person is not available.

3.5 Challenges Ahead

Important Business challenges:

- Meet customer expectations on service and facility offered by the bank.
- Customer retention.
- Managing the spread and sustain the operating profit.
- Retaining the current market share in the industry and the improving the same.
- Completion from other players in the banking industry.

Other Important Operational Challenges:

- Frequent challenges in technologies used focusing up grades in hardware and software, attending to that implementation issues and timely roll out.
- Managing technology, security and business risks.
- System re-engineering to enable. Defined and implemented efficient processes to be able to reap benefits off technology to its fullest potential.
- Upgrading the skill of work force spread across the country.

With the opening of economy, deregulation, mergers and acquisition of banks, implementation of BASLE II norms, disinvestment of government holding in banks, the competition is going to be increased from new banks and merged entities. This will also open up new opportunities for introduction of a new products and services. A definite trend is emerging as to consolidation of the banking system, sharing of ATM networks and services, Tie ups with insurance companies, other billing organizations like mobile operators, electricity and telephone bills and bank for cross selling of various products and services.

3.6 How to Meet the Challenges?

At corporate level to meet the challenges, various initiated have been taken and implementation is in process beside up gradation of Data Center facilities:

1. Centralization of functions

- Inward clearing Data uploading and processing.
- Check Book Issues.
- MIS-On-Line Monitoring/Generation of statement by controlling offices.
- Audit from the Remote Location.
- Sending Mails and statement of accounts to customers & completion of non-mandatory field in newly opened accounts.

2. Single Window System.
3. Revised Account opening from for capturing complete customer/Account data as per CBS requirement.
4. Call center for Customers.
5. Customer Relationship Management (CRM) Application.
6. Data Warehousing.

3.7 Immediate Focus

To facilitate successful implementation of the above initiative, intensive efforts are to be undertaken by all of us on following issues:

1. Completion of correct MIS details in all accounts and SRM's.
2. Customer/Account data completion/correction.
3. Customer-ID crystallization.
4. Aggressive marketing of Internet Banking & Debit Card products to increase share of delivery channels transaction.
5. Skill up gradation & increase in awareness of all staff member.
6. Strict compliance of Circular & Guidance available online (CBSINFO)/Messages issued through scrolling ticker on login page.

Present slowdown in rollover must be put to full use to have concrete action on these fronts.

3.8 Conclusion

Indian public sector banks that hold around 75 per cent of market share do have taken initiative in the field of IT. They are moving towards the centralized database and decentralize decisions making process. They possess enviable quality manpower. Awareness and appreciation of IT are very much there. What is needed is a 'big push' the way it was given in the post nationalization period for expansionary activities.

IT and India have become synonymous. Whether India becomes a destination for outsourcing or it becomes a development center is matter of debate. As far as banking industry in India is concerned it can be said that although the Indian banks may not be as technologically advanced as their counterparts in the developed world, they are following the majority of international trends on the IT front. The strength of Indian banking lie in withering storms and rising up to the expectations from all the quarters – catching up with all the global trends is a matter of time.

References

Bank Quest (various issues).

Information Technology (various issues).

Balasubramanya, S. (2002), IT Wave Breaks over Banking, *The City*, Aug.-Sept.

Biswas, S, 'Information Technology in Service Sector- A Vision for India', available at www.tifac.org.in

Gupta, S.C. (2003), Banking Industry Vision 2010, *IBA Committee Report*, November.

Leeladhar, V. 'Contemporary and Future Issues in Indian Banking', Available at www.rbi.org.

Maheshwari, S.N. *Banking Law and Practice*, Kalyani Publishers.

Nayyar, *Taxmann's Banking Law Practice in India*, Taxmann Publishers.

Patrick R Anil (2003), The Tech Factor in Banking Technology in Banking, *Network Magazine*, May.

Ramanathan, A. (1998), Financial Liberalization and Economic Development – The Theory and Experience, *IEJ*, Vol. 46, No.1.

Rangarajan, S.C. (2000), Financial Sector Reforms: Managing Changes, *PNB, M.R.*, Vol. 18, No. 11.

Rangarajan, S.C. (2000), Financial Sector Reforms: The Indian Experience, *RBI Bulletin*, July.

Varshney, P. N., *Banking Law and Practice*, Kalyani Publishers.

4

Application of Information Technology in Banking

Seema Kapoor and Deepak Dhingra

4.1 Introduction

With globalization trends world over, it is difficult for any nation, big or small, developed or developing, to remain isolated from what is happening around. For a country like India which is one of the most promising emerging markets, such isolation is nearly impossible. More particularly, in the area of Information Technology where India has definitely an edge over its competitors, remaining away or uninformed of the world trend is untenable. IT and India have become synonymous. Information Technology shrunk the world as a result of which time & distance have become non-entities to a large extent. The IT has changed the structure of Indian banking. The concept of banking has drastically changed from a business dealing with money transactions alone to a business related to information on financial transactions. The technology has been the main facilitator in the process of transformation. The precise impact, technology had on the banking industry since 1980's is difficult to assess, because of the intimacy of relationship between the industry and technology, it is impossible to separate the two. As for as baking industry in India is concerned, it can be said that although the Indian banks may not be as technologically advanced as their counterparts in the develop world, they are following the majority of international trends on IT front.

IT has a lot of influence on banking sector. The new methods of banking practices on account of IT ensure which service besides reducing cost in baking sector. Computerization in banking is taking place all over the world. The purpose of computerization is to bring technology to counter and enable to employees to have information as their fingertips. This enabled the banks to offer better quality of services to customers besides ensuring accurate information at a faster rate on banking transaction. Thus, the adoption of IT in banking has undergone several changes with the passage of time. Today, IT has become inseparable segment of banking organization.

4.2 Need for IT Adoption in Banking

Information Technology has a significant influence on the banking sector. In fact, it started a new era in the banking operation. The application of IT in banks reduced the scope of conventional banking with manual operations. The banking sector is still undergone changes with innovation. It seems several lessons have emerged in the banking on account of this magical technology. Some important lessons in the contacts of IT with reference to banking sector are listed below.

- The increase in investment in banking sector has forced to switch on to automation of existing processes.
- Cost sharing between customers and products and its analysis forced banks to go for IT. Costs in banking are shared across products and even across customers. An investment that might have a positive impact on one customer base or product may have the desired impact on the overall cost.base.
- Banking services may be a class of services for which demand and supply creates additional demand. Banks have recognized that they need to offer the conveniences of newer technology to retain their existing customers.
- The mix effect of technology in banking reflect the fact that technology can replace simple repetitive functions such as the basic calculations and internally oriented back office support functions that were automated initially.

Therefore, investment in new technology must be made to modernize the existing banks operations. The adoption of Information Technology also helps them to face competition and new challenges to meet the customer expectation in the contacts of globalization.

4.3 Technological Advance in Banking

With competition as the buzzword among banks, all categories of banks have been investing on computerization and use of advanced communication networks. The directive by Central Vigilance Commission (CVC) to banks to achieve 100 per cent computerization has imparted urgency to the process to the process of technological advancement. While new private sector banks, foreign banks and a few older private sector banks have been enjoying a head start in adopting "core banking solutions", PSU (Public Sector Banks) banks too have fallen in line rather vigorously. Besides, all PSU Banks, except eight, had achieved 100 per cent full / computerization as on March 31, 2005. Of 27 PSU Banks, as many as nine had 100 per cent computerization branches; 19 had more than 50 per cent.

Technological innovation both externally and internally brought about changes in banking sector. The external innovation can be found in product and service offering. Similarly internal innovation is found in operational functions of bank. The application of information technology in banking sector resulted in the development of different concepts of banking sector such as E-banking, Internet-banking, Online Banking, Telephone Baking, Automated Teller Machine, Universal Banking and Investment Banking etc. with quick electronic services to the dynamic customers of information society.

4.3.1 Online Banking: The Online Banking service allows customers to manage their money from any type of browser device including mobile phones, internet enabled T.V and even small hand electronic organizers. Using a PC to access are account, transfer funds, pay creditors and check if payment has been made etc. is called online banking. It allows customer to have constant access to accounts at any time of day or night.

The Bankers Automated Clearing System (BACS) has been introduced in online banking to reduce paper cost and the risk of security. As we are aware information is a vital factor in running a successful business. Service link is offered by online banking as a solution to problems business may encounter when dealing with all financial methods. Service link brings you up-to-date information about your online bank accounts directly to your desktop. The window based software links your office PC to the bank so you can have access to your account information and carry out a range of banking activities by using a private password your account balance will be shown as the close of business the previous working day. The projected cleared balances for the current day are also shown. Online banking ensures the following services:

- Checking the position of account
- Moving the spare cash into and interest bearing account
- Making high value payments without risk

4.3.2 E-banking: Banks are using the electronic technology to meet the ever-increasing competition in banking which has converted the traditional brick and mortar banking into Electronic Banking (E-banking). E-banking as per as information technology is concerned may be identified with three channels viz., ATM, Internet Banking and Tele Banking. These channels can supplement each other in ensuring the convenient way of delivering banking services. With increasing consumer demand, banks have to constantly think of innovative customized services to remain competitive. E-banking is an innovative tool for banks that is fast becoming a necessity. It is a successful strategic weapon for banks to remain profitable in a volatile and competitive market place of today. Banks are in a position to lead consumer views, as well as to cater to existing demand. Clearly, despite the threats posed by non-bank financial intermediaries, there is enormous opportunity for far-sighted banks to reap the reward available from E-banking.

4.3.3 Automated Teller Machine (ATM): The cash machine or Automated Teller Machine (ATM) as it is more formerly non is the most visible and perhaps most revolutionary element of virtual banking revolution. ATMs are self service vendor machine that help the banks to provide round the clock banking services to their customers at convenient places without visiting to the bank premises. They enable the banks to transact more business by offering various services in cost effective way on one side and to get more customer satisfaction on the other. To avail the ATM services customers are provided with ATM Card, which is a small plastic card with magnetic strip, containing information about the name of bank, name of the customer, card number, validity period, and signature panel. The magnetic strip contains information about the customer which enables the banks to verify the identity when the card is inserted at the slot provided in ATM. The following functions can be performed on ATM.

- Withdrawal of cash up to a particular limit.
- Deposit of cash, cheques or drafts. The ATM will immediately printout receipt for the same
- Updated balance of customer is appeared on the screen and will also be printed on a transaction slip.
- Transfer of money from one account to another account can be done.
- A customer through ATM can obtain mini account statement.
- A customer can ask for cheque book / detailed account statement through ATM. These are mailed to customers later on by bank employee.
- A customer can maintain a joint account for which he can get an additional card on the name of the other joint account holder.
- All the branches of bank are provided with an on-site, on-line ATM. A customer can operate his account any ATM of the bank across India. It is a concept of anywhere banking.

Some of the observations made by banking expert about the significant role of ATMs in banking services are shown here under. Keith Taylor, senior Vice-president; Financial Solutions division, NCR corporation, expressed that "India is one of the world's lowest users of ATMs". He says that people still prefer cash and cheque transaction. He pointed out that the worldwide installed base of ATMs is a over 1.1 Million unit. In India from a small installed base of 500 ATMs in 1998, it has grown to nearly 7,500 ATMs. He also expressed that ATM penetration in India is only 7 per mission, while in case of developed countries such as in USA it is 1200 ATMs per million, China 44 ATMs per million, Thailand 100 per million and Philippines 60 per million.

The ATMs are emerging as the most useful tool to ensure, "Any-Time Banking" and "Any-where Banking" or "Any-Time Money". While the benefits of ATM are immense, the cost of ATM, though has come, down, it still prohibitive. An ATM costs between Rs. 8-10 lakh. If a bank has to install 100 ATMs it should spend at least Rs.8-10crs. Added to this, is the maintenance cost. Today ant electronic device attracts and annual maintaining cost of Rs.8-12 per cent of capital cost. Besides this banks have to incur expenditure on the rent for retail outlet, its ambience and on security personnel etc. While many Public Sector Banks have gone on a big way in opening ATMs there is a need for sufficient examination of their economic viability. Already there is experience that the hits per ATM are less than 200 resulting in no big gain for either the bank of customer. The average usage of ATMs in Europe was 3300 withdrawals per machine per month in 1999. Sweden has reported exceptional high in hits with an average of 10156 withdrawals per ATM per month. India with more population density should show a higher average hit per day and this emerges as a critical factor in the overall ATM strategy towards making the whole business idea profitable.

With the increasing pressures on spreads, banks have no alternative but to resort to cost cutting exercise in whatever way feasible and ATM is considered as one of the acceptable strategies for cost control.

The rationale for banks introducing ATMs in 1970s, Telephone banking in 1980s and now Internet Banking was to deliver their products More Cheaply than Traditional Branch Networks which are loaded with expensive staff.

Private Sector Banks are going ahead with aggressive ATM plans particularly off-site (away from branch) for wider reach with lower cost. They are also targeting ATM deployment in the top corporate offices or staff colonies – not only for the salary accounts but also for a piece of the Corporate Pie and also to get the find following benefits.

- Reduces overheads.
- Minimized use of costly consumable like cheque – leaves etc.
- Can lead to increased profitability by reducing costs per transaction imperative in an intensely competitive environment.
- With increase in number of ATM cards and usage, transaction cost will decline substantially.
- Can advertise Bank's products on screen – cross selling loans, insurance, credit cards etc.
- Revenue earning stream – through sale of tickets, bill payments income tax collections etc.

The success of cost reduction thorough the ATM depends on may factor:

- Right location of the ATMs
- Optimum population of ATMs at each center
- Provision of maximum facilities at the ATMs
- Customer education
- Making the customer habitual of using ATMs
- Involvement, preparedness and willingness of staff at all levels to make the program a success.

Any new ideas is greeted with resistance world over and ATM is no different in this regard, It is reported that even in USA, the ATMs in the initial stages were am unwelcome curiosity. There is thus a dire need to increase the usage of ATM by proper education of staff and customer. To ward off the problem of poor hits and to make the investment viable banks enter into shared network agreement. **Swadhan** is the name given to the shared ATM Network of Public Sector Banks and some private banks. The Indian Bank Association introduced Swadhan, a system of shared payment network.

P.C. Narayan, President of Global Trust Bank, classifies shared ATM networks into two kinds, viz. "Parent Child" and "Peer to peer'. A good example of parent child would be a large sized bank. Which has a lot of ATMs and which it could of to smaller banks to be a large bank coming together to build a national ATM network. All ATMs in generally have the sharing network with other banks. This would be mutually beneficial both for small and big banks, while big banks can benefit from their strength of resources, small banks need not commit their capital to upgrade their technology.

4.3.4 Internet Banking: Internet Banking is the latest and the cheapest technology introduced in the banking industry. It is acknowledged that the Internet has already had a profound effect on delivery of financial services and this likely to bring more radical changes. At the basic level, interknit banking can mean the setting up of a web-page by a bank to give information about its products and services. At an advance level, it involves provision of facilities such as accessing accounts, fund transfer, and buying financial products or services online. This is called "Transactional Online Banking".

In general Internet Banking refers to the use of internet as a delivery channel for the banking services, including traditional services, such as opening an account or transferring funds among different accounts, as well as new banking services such as electronic bill presentation and payment, which allows the customers to pay and receive the bills on a bank's website.

There are two ways two offers Internet Banking. First, an existing bank with physical offices can establish a web-site and offer internet banking in addition to its traditional delivery channel. Second, a bank may be established as a "branchless", "Internet only", or "Virtual Bank". Further internet banking sites offer financial services products to customer in three basic formats:

- **Informational only:** Informational only presents online information about the different banks services and products to the customers as well as the general public and may include unsecured e-mail contact, with no customer identification or verification required.
- **Information Exchange:** Information Exchange Customer

Information such as name, address and account information may be collected or displayed, with possible secure e-mail and/or data transfer, with verification of customer identification required. No financial transactions are to be made.

- **Transactional:** Transactional customer account information enquiry, financial transactions such as transfer of funds, payment of bill, application for loans and a variety of other financial transactions, with strong customer authentication required.

When it was introduced for the first time, Internet Banking was used mainly as an information presentation medium in which banks marketed their products and services on their web sites with the development of asynchronous technologies and secured electronic transitions technologies, however more banks have come forward to use internet banking both as a transactional as well as an informational medium.

A successful Internet Banking solution offers:

- Exceptional rate on savings CDS, and IRAS
- Checking with no monthly fee, free bill payment and rebates on ATM surcharges
- Credit card with low rates
- Easy online applications for all accounts, including personal loans and mortgages
- 24 hour account access
- Quality customer service with personal attention

Internet Banking is a cost-effective delivery channel for financial institutions. All the transactions are encrypted, using sophisticated multi-layer security architecture, including fire walls and filters. Firewall is a protection device to shield a vulnerable area from some form of danger. In Internet, a firewall system (a computer or a router) set up specifically, to shield a web from outside. Typically, this allows insiders (bank) to have full access to services on the outside, while granting access into the internal system, selectively based on log-in name & password.

Internet Banking is somewhat different from PC banking. PC

banking is transactions through a PC at one's office/home, which is connected to the branch through a modem. PC banking is available only when branch is open and is available only through that PC. But, Internet Banking enables to do the same through any PC connected to the Internet, from anywhere in the world.

Internet Banking is in its nascent stage in India. Only the ICICI Bank, HDFC Bank, Citi Bank and Federal Bank are offering full-fledged internet banking. There after UTI Bank, Bank of Punjab & IDBI Bank have also started internet banking services.

4.3.5 Telephone Banking: The banks are aiming to make them more accessible by introducing telephone banking. Telephone Banking refers to dialing one telephone number using a telephone to access the account, transfer funds, request statements or cheque book simply by following recorded message and touching the keys on your phone. It allows the customers to check account at a convenient time and get simple things done without visiting bank premises. Telephone banking aims at providing 24 hr. services that is fast, convenient and secured for all customers. In the modern society everyone has to access to telephone. Registering for telephone banking cost nothing although there is a small transactions charge for making bill payment and frequent usage charges.

4.4 Banking through Mobile Phones

The mobile owing customers of major Indian banks particularly NPSBs are now be able to give their approval for the clearance of Cheque with the help of two-way communication technology development. The two-way text messaging system technology allows customers to submit requests and get answers from the bank on their mobiles phones about banking transaction like clearance cheques or credit balance. The HDFS Bank, ICICI Bank and CITI Bank are offering Mobile Banking in India in association with Cellular Service Provider such as Orange Tel, Air Tel, Sky Cell and BPL Mobile. Though this access is available only through SMS technology, all of them are graduating to WAP-enabled mobile companies.

Internet banking including mobile banking will emerge as one more channel of distribution for banks. Mobile banking is all set to explore, because of growing no. of mobile phones available across the globe. Even in countries such as US, where Internet and PC penetration are very high, the access to internet banking is very limited. Compare this with India's low PC penetration, low net access, high cost of browsing, lack of computerized and networked bank branches and security concerns. Most certainly, traditional banking will survive in India, even with the emergence of Internet Banking.

4.5 Outsourcing and Status of Banking Industry

Outsourcing is one of the major trends in IT industry. It is also the most controversial, talked about & published trend. Outsourcing is the transfer or delegation to and external service provider, the operation and day to day management of a business process. The customers receive a service that performs a distinct business function that fits into the customers overall business operation. The magnitude of outsourcing has increased considerably resulting in a widening scope of services in all spheres of activities. As technology has evolved, outsourcing of information, services has become more common. In the recent years the Indians ITES-BPO market has been notching up record growth rates and during 2004-05 the industry achieved the momentum of around of 44.4 per cent with revenue touching US$ 5.8 billion. The industry has shown a compound annual growth rate of 56.4 per cent over 2000-05 phase and remains the largest employment generating segment within the country. The global demand for outsourcing and off shoring from American and British firms alone is forecast to rise from $ 10 billion now to may be $ 60 billion by 2008, 40 per cent of which is likely to be in banking & insurance.

4.5.1 Need for Outsourcing: Outsourcing is more than just a cost cutting initiative. Some of its benefits are:

- Lowering cost and maximizing efficiencies enabling focus on core competencies.

- Increasing business productivity of the staff
- Accessing best of breed talent and technology
- Improve quality of services and finance related data and analysis

The banking and financial service sector is witnessing a concerted move towards BPO as a strategic option. This industry is ideally suited for outsourcing, given large transactions volume, structured decision-making and reliance on rules set process. In the past BPO was limited to back office operations in banking sector but more recently BPO providers have expanded their offerings to mid-and front-office offerings like credit card payment processing, cash management and mortgage origination and lending. Citi Bank Employees over 2,500 people in Mumbai and Chennai where they handle finance and loan process. Since BPO reduces management complexity, it enables top managers to re-focus on issues which are really important, viz., building market share, protecting the bottom line, exploring and entering new markers etc. it can be used as a tool for turning strategy into delivered business results

4.6 Problem Associated with Technology

Whatever we spoke about the adoption of new technology, it does not mean that all new technology implementation to improve the process and system brings positive results. Major obstacle and risks associated with innovative technology are:

- Increase cash flows are not sufficient to cover the cost associated with the implementation of new technology.
- New technology increases the capacity that could results in excess capacity in the bank
- Another problem bank space when they bring in new technology is integration of traditional and new system.
- Innovative technology may result in cost overrun and cost control problems.

4.7 Key Areas for Consideration

Information technology would be the navigator of

transformation process in any bank. However, the following issues need to be addressed by banks while implementing the technology up gradation.

- The back office tasks such as end of day (EOD) should be run in a centralized mode and operating staff at branches would be relieved of this pressure.
- Central deposit of data would enable costing and prizing of product and services. Individual banks can innovate new products and services to match the changing expectation of customer.
- A systematic study of different demographic and economic characteristics of targeted customers should be useful. Customer information system on one had and online access to his transactions on the other, the management would be able to device and early warning signal system for all types of borrower accounts. Such information should facilitate effective control to being down none-performing assets.
- For providing better customer service the bank shall have to weight all the delivery choices from cost-benefit perspective. Changing customer expectations need to be given due consideration while getting into ATMs or debit/credit cards.
- Adequate trained staff should be there for proper implementation of technology.
- With increase mass or retail banking the customer has undergone a change in their expectations and aspirations. The changes of this kind should be recognized as important ingredients in the implementation of core banking solution.
- In Indian context typical profile of clerical and managerial staff in public sector banks is one the wrong side of 40 years and top and senior management on the wrong side of 50 years. If these banks have to attract new and young customer, infusion of younger staff is necessary as the new players of technology made the older and elder feel more incompetent

4.8 Conclusion

Information technology allows the baking industry to

establish a direct link to customers. Bank customers can bank online, including viewing their account balances, and transaction histories, paying bills, transferring funds between accounts, requesting credit cared advances and ordering checks.

The banking industry also recognized that the Internet must be secure to achieve a high level of confidence with both customers and businesses. Internet banking creates new challenges for banks, which must be addressed o before the adoption of this new technology. The regulator would also be concerned with whether the nature of products and services offered are within regulatory framework and weather the transactions do not camouflage money-laundering operations. In such a scenario, the thrust if regulatory thinking has been to ensure that while the banks remain efficient and cost effective, they must be aware of the risk involved and have proper built-in-safeguards, machinery and systems to manage the emerging risk.. The domestic standard of banking has to be in conformity with the well-known international standards and in the near future international dealings from India would be a reality, which are presently not liberal enough. No system or institution can hope to benchmark it against international standards without making optimal use of technology. They can be no doubt about the enormous potential and emancipated opportunities offered by advances in technology. However, there are perquisites and preparations which have to be made before the fill benefits of the technology can be harvested.

References

ATM Transactions Pip Credit Cards, *Economic Times*, May 31, 2003.

Banu, Hasan (2004), Outsourcing Marketing; A New Mantra in Banking Industry, *Southern Economist*, Sept. 1, pp. 7-8.

BPOs to Provide Jobs in New Areas, *The Tribune*, June 21, 2006.

Chhabra, Sangeeta (2006), Business Process Outsourcing–Finance & Accounting: An Introduction, *The Management Accountant*, Vol. 41, No.8, pp. 605-609.

EPW Research Foundation (2006), Increasing Concentration of Banking Operations, *Economic & Political Weekly*, Vol. XLI, No.11, pp.

1113 – 1117.

Gupta, Ankur (2006), Data Protection in Consumer E-banking, *Journal of Internet Banking and Commerce*, Vol.11, No.1.

Laxman, G. (2005), ATM Services and Perceptions of Users; A Case Study of Andhra Bank, *Southern Economist*, Vol. 44, No.5, pp. 16-20.

Malhotra, Pooja and Singh Balwinder (2005), New Revolution in the Indian Banking Industry; Internet Banking, *Punjab Journal of Business Studies*, Vol.1, No.1, pp. 75-86.

Marwaha, Rajesh (2005), Infotrends in Indian Banking Industry, *Punjab Journal of Business Studies*, Vol. 1, No.1, pp. 94 – 101.

Prasad, P.S.R. (2006), Cost Benefit Analysis (Automated Teller Machine), *The Management Accountant,* Vol.6, No.8, pp. 622-627.

Rahul Sachitanand (2003), ATM Will Deliver Much More, *The Economic Times*, Feb. 13.

Unnithan, C.R. and Swatman, P. (2001), E-banking Adaptations and Dot.Com violability - A Comparison of Australian and Indian Experience in Banking Sector, Working Paper, School of Management & Information System, Deakin University, No.14.

5

Plastic Money

Preety Sharma and Pooja Mehta

When we use the term "Card Technologies" what do we mean? The easy answer is any technology that can be placed on a card. What is a card? Typically we think of our credit or bank card but there are other sized or materials used for different applications. The card can be made of plastic (polyester, PVC, or some other material) or paper, card or even amalgamation of materials. The common point is that the card is used to provide "access" to something and it includes some form of AIDC (Automatic Identification and Data Capture) technology,

Plastic cards also known as plastic currency involving electronic device in their functioning is gaining popularity as a convenient mode of payment. Broadly defined, electronic payment is a financial exchange that takes place online between buyers and sellers. The contents of this exchange is in some form of digital financial instruments such as encrypted credit card numbers or debit card numbers backed by a bank or an intermediary. Three factors that are stimulating interest among financial institutions in electronic payment – decreasing cost, reduced operational and processing cost and increasing online commerce.

5.1 The Technologies

So what are the technologies that we use with cards? Here is a list of the common ones along with a brief description of each:

5.1.1 Bar Code: A printed technology using "black and white" bars to encode the data. From early beginning of barcodes that could only encode a few digits, today there have been over 250 barcodes invented. Luckily, many of them have fallen by a wayside and we only concentrate on a few of these. Linear barcodes that we see everyday on all our retail purchases are perhaps the most pervasive; however, the new two-dimensional barcodes that include error correction and detection are becoming more used. Large amount of data can be stored on a small symbol, making them very useful for making small objects. The cost of printing barcode is very low but they cannot be changed without replacing the label.

5.1.2 Barium Ferrite: These are some high power magnets that are buried in a plastic card to form a pattern. This type of card was very popular in assess control cards in 1980s. problems with the cards included the extra thickness card needed to embed the magnets and the erasure of conventional magnetic strips.

5.1.3 Contact Smart Card: smart cards are credit card sized plastic cards that contain relatively large amount of information in an embedded micro-chip. Smart card differs from magnetic stripe card in two ways: the amount of information that can be stored is much greater and some smart cards can be re-programmed to add, delete or re-arrange data.

There are several terms used to identify cards with integrated circuits embedded in them. The term "chip card", "integrated circuit" and "smart card" really all refer to the same thing.

There are two types of smart card. The first is really a "dumb card" in that it only contains memory. These cards are used to store information. Example of a "dumb card" is the memory that is plugged into personal computer. The second type of card is a true "smart card" where a microprocessor is embedded into the card along with memory. Now the card actually has the ability to make decisions about the data stored on the card. Smart cards are the technology of choice when fairly large database must travel with an individual or an object. For instance a version of smart card technology is used to record service histories for automobiles. The data travels on a small tag on the owner's key ring. It can be re-programmed, updated and accessed whenever the vehicle is serviced with any of that company's dealers. The possible benefits of an acceptance of smart card technology depend upon the application in use. However, the ability to move large amounts of data with little or no increase in security of the data will lead to many new applications being created that we haven't even begun to think about.

5.1.4 Contact Less Smart Card: The contact less version of a smart card does not have gold plated contacts visible on the card. The contact less card uses a technology to pass data between the card and the reader without any physical contact being made. The advantage to this card less system is that there are no contacts to wear out, no chance of an electric shock coming through the contacts and destroying the integrated circuit and the knowledge that the components are completely embedded in the plastic with no external connections.

5.1.5 Data glyphs: This is a proprietary form of 2D barcode that allows for large amounts of the data to be stored in a small space.

5.1.6 Embossed plastic cards: After the original metal plate, this becomes the choice of technology for many applications. Even today there are still applications that rely on this technology. All that is involved is the plastic card which has been embossed using a method of pushing the characters into the plastic. This requires the use of an embossable plastic (PVC etc). The data is ready by passing a heavy roller across a carbon impregnated paper to get an impression of the embossing.

5.1.7 Hologram: It is an image recorde3d using laser light which as you move the image. It is used on many cards as a form of security as reproduction of the hologram is not easy. Size ranges from small image to a full card image.

5.1.8. Magnetic Stripe: Magnetic Stripe technology is everywhere. We use card with magnetic strips on them everyday without even thinking about it. The technology has been with us for many years, but there are still many new things going on in the industry. This system used a stored value on the magnetic stripe which was read and rewritten every time the card was used. With the advent of new technologies many people have predicted the demise of the magnetic stripe. However, with the investment in the current infrastructure this is not likely to be anytime soon. Magnetic Stripe technology provides the ideal solution to many aspects of our life. It is very important and readily adaptable to many functions.

5.1.9 Optical memory card: Optical memory card uses a technology similar to the one used for music or CD ROMs. A penal of the "gold colored" laser sensitive material is laminated in the card and is used to store the information. The material is comprised of several layers that react when a laser light is directed at them. The laser burns a tiny hole (2.25 microns in diameters) in the material which can then be sensed by a low power laser during the read cycle. The presence or absence of the burn spot indicates a 'one' or a 'zero'. Because the material is actually burned during the write cycle, the media is a write once read many (WORM) media and the data is non volatile (not lost when power is removed). The optical card can currently store between 4 and 6.6MB of data which gives the ability to store graphical images such as photographs, logos, fingerprints, X-Rays etc. The biggest uses of optical technology today are: medical/Healthcare; prepaid debit cards; cargo manifests; Admission pass season tickets; Auto maintenance records and retail purchase cards.

5.1.10 PCMCIA: These are now called PC card. A credit card form factor card that has an edge connector and is plugged into computers and computing devices. Various standards exist for different application but primary uses are memory, modems, LAN cards and hard disks.

5.1.11 Secure Magnetic: A form of magnetic stripe that provides a method of securing the data on the magnetic stripe. Several different proprietary methods are available, each using a different method of tying data on the stripe to a particular physical stripe or card.

5.1.12 Wigand: It is a method of embedding wires into a card. The wires are sensed into a card. The wires are sensed by a magnetic pulse to provide a binary encodation of data.

5.2 Drawbacks

The virtual explosion of credit cards, however, is not without problems. As money and security become more digital and are transmitted across more devices. Channels and borders, the security of the transaction becomes increasingly critical.

Recently a customer purchased jewels worth Rs. 80,000 and offered the plastic card for payment. On verification, it was found to be a fake card. Before he could be nabbed, he quietly slipped from the shop leaving behind the jewellary and the card. This is not an isolated case.

Industry sources recall intriguing instances. Consider this: you are checking out of a hotel and decide to settle your dues with your credit card. You hand the card to the bearer, who brings it back with the charge slip.

Have you ever paused to think what paused to think what frauds could have taken place in the meantime? Your card could have been swiped more than once (manually), your data could have been captured and passed on, the card could have been altered.... So many things can happen in a matter of few minutes and they are not unknown yet. The card holder blindly signs the charge slip and walks away, only to find some discrepancy in his statement at a later date.

Till this date, no foolproof method has been established to clamp down on such manipulations, as even the most sophisticated fraud control systems or neural networks depend on the integrity and carefulness of the people who use them. As simple as that...

Huge sums have been spent on the automation of authorization and monitoring systems and electronic data capture at the point of sale to deter scams, but the manual swiping machine continues to exist. Criminals are known to be continually scheming for ways to beat the system. They counterfeit and alter cards; dishonest merchants find ways to defraud bank by creating false drafts an real card holder account numbers, submit bogus applications or application information to an issuer with the intention of establishing a credit line and obtaining credit cards for fraudulent use. Considering the number of applications processed by the issuer every month, detecting fraudulent applications could be difficult. Despite authorities incorporating various security features to prevent or scam, fraudulent transactions continue to take place.

Two key challenges in a digital payment environment are to extend the same security that exist in a physical world to virtual transaction and ensure privacy to users. The security concerns have mushroomed over the years. In a recent move, the UK banking industry has moved forward with a chip and pin technology to combat spiraling credit card frauds. In spite of all these measures, reports show that the circulation of fake or counterfeit cards has been on the rise in UK.

5.3 Conclusion

Isn't it convenient to carry your credit card when on a buying spree than move around with hard cash? Exactly, and this is what most of us do. Whether in buying jewellary or checking out of a hotel, the plastic card comes in handy, rather than currency bundles. In fact most people boast at more than one card, purportedly as a 'status symbol'. On the other hand the banking industry's survey showed that the credit card fraud reached £425 million last year and was estimated at £800 million by 2005, mostly due to counterfeit or fake cards in circulation.

So when you hold out your card next time, bear in mind that plastic card is worth more than money within the context of card abuse.

6

Internet Payments: The Role of Central Bank

Neetu Gupta

What role could, or should, Central Banks play in the Internet payments industry? It is a difficult question, as it is not yet clear how, and to what extent, such industry will develop, and whether governments will allow such developments. According to some, Internet payments are a matter of private initiative, and the Central Bank should play no role at all. They dream of an unregulated world, where multiple currencies, as well as baskets of currencies and other assets, are equally accepted as means of payment. Others point out at the risks of such a scenario, and at the increased volatility and unpredictability of financial prices that it could cause.

Economic theory is not helpful either. Even though the payment system as a whole is crucial to economic stability, and is, indeed, one of the main concerns of Central Banks, it is seldom taken into account in economic models. It is normally considered as part of the institutional context or analyzed through its effects, mainly on the banking system, the monetary and financial markets, the instruments of monetary policy. The problem with this approach is that it is static, as it considers the payment system and the institutional context as given. Furthermore, if the traditional Central Banking institutional model is clearly becoming rapidly outdated, elaborating a new one poses several problems. Globalization and the growing integration of national payment systems, as well as the increasing amounts of payments handled through private clearing houses requires an international approach, at least on a G-10 level. However, as Mr. Padoa

Schioppa, of the Bank of Italy, says, "the road to define a new institutional model must be different from the ones adapted in the past. At the beginning of this century, an agreement on how to manage a monetary system based on currency and deposits was only reached after a financial and monetary crisis. It would be extremely dangerous to pass through a similar learning process today, not least because payment systems in the industrialized world would amplify the problems of any single market operator, diffusing its effects to the whole economy".

Traditionally, Central Banks have four duties: they manage monetary policy, they supervise the payment system, they promulgate regulations, and, in many countries, they supervise the banking system as a whole. Each of there roles is going to be affected, in a way or another.

As a **monetary authority**, the Central Bank will have to adapt its procedures to the new context. I believe that its ability to control monetary aggregates will not be seriously thwarted, at least in the short and medium run. Internet payment instruments are indeed a new financial instrument, significantly different from traditional ones, but many innovations have changed and are changing the banking and financial industry. Furthermore, current and projected volumes for the next few years are not large enough to have significant macroeconomic effects. Probably changes and adaptations will be required in the econometric models used to predict the trends of economic variables, as variables such as the velocity of money, capital mobility, etc. could be affected.

Other effects could derive as a result of the current trend of institutional de-specialization. Today the monopoly held by banks over the payment industry is increasingly being threatened by non banks. Department store credit cards are an example of such new competitors. Internet payment instruments, if provided by non banking institutions, could increase this tendency. As Central Banks enforce monetary policy through their "special" relationship with banks, a decreased importance of such institutions could decrease its effectiveness.

The role of the Central Bank as **supervisor of the payment system** will be affected too. Central banks can take part in the payment system in three ways:

- through consulting and moral suasion it can spur market operators to adopt certain behaviours, which it believes to be positive for efficiency and stability
- it can promulgate rules which bind market operators to certain behaviours (ex. legal reserve requirements)
- it can choose to offer directly certain services, if the other two options are impossible or too costly (ex. the supply of currency).

It is yet unclear what approach the Central Banks will adapt towards Internet payment instruments. It is likely that, as long as Internet payment instruments are growing, Central Banks will refrain from imposing limits and regulations, to avoid impairing growth. And it is quite unlikely that Central Banks will ever offer Internet payment services. Before deciding to what extent Central Banks should be involved, a serious analysis of the effects of such instruments on the international settlement system should be done. Even if Internet payment instruments target the retail sector of the payment market, and therefore do not imply the same systemic risk of large value payments, at an aggregate level they could still become relevant. Furthermore, current international settlement systems are not made to handle vast amounts of small payments. In the medium term, new ways of settling such payments should be devised.

As a **regulator**, and as an advisor to the government, the Central Bank is faced with several significant questions:

- How to preserve the integrity of the payment system? Who is responsible for settlement? What settlement system should be provided?
- How to protect customers from bankruptcy of a supplier of payment instruments? How to treat, from a legal point of view, the new digital instruments?
- How to deal with the international implications of the Internet?

- How to ensure competition and transparency?
- What, if any, standards should payment instruments meet?
- How to avoid that the new instruments be used for tax evasion or money laundering?

As a **supervisor of the banking system**, the Central Bank has to rethink its special relationship with banks. As already said, institutional de-specialisation currently implies that banking institutions face more and more competition from non-banks. The industry of Internet payments is a typical example, as most of the companies who are offering payment services are non-banks. Whereas, in the past, it was sufficient to monitor banking institutions to guarantee the stability of the payment system, today too many payments are not being intermediated by banks any more. Therefore, the scope for offering settlement services and credit of last resort only to banks is becoming less and less relevant. In the future, if Internet payment instruments, as well as several other payment instruments managed by non-banks, are going to take off, it is foreseeable that the regulations applied to banks will be extended to all the companies who wish to operate in the payment industry. This would avoid unfair competition (if non-banks are not subject to the same rules as banks, they have an unfair advantage) and instability. This is the opinion expressed by the Payment System Task Force of the EU.

Furthermore, traditionally Central Banks only monitor national banks. The development of Euromarkets has pushed the Central Banks of G10 Countries to extend their supervision to foreign subsidiaries of national banks. Internet payment instruments are a further step forward, being completely independent of physical location. It is possible for national companies to sell their products abroad, and for foreign ones to compete in the national market just like national operators. Suppose a European Bank located in Cayman Island starts selling US$ denominated payment instruments to customers in Japan. Which Central Bank, if any, should be responsible?

The problem is even more serious than for other international assets and financial instruments, as Internet payment instruments target families and consumers, and not just financial operators. This means that there is a stronger "*need for protection*" from risks.

It is, however, difficult for a Central Bank to extend its powers to foreign companies, as this would infringe the sovereignty of other States. There are, however, ways to exert some kind of control. For instance, Central Banks can use their powers of moral suasion. In the case of Internet payment instruments, Central Banks could decide to provide those operators who accept to submit themselves to Central Bank controls with a digital certificate proving the stability of the operator. Such certificates would tell customers anywhere in the world that they are accepting a payment instrument which has been declared secure by an independent, non-profit driven institution such as the Central Bank. Users would quickly learn how to distinguish between certified suppliers and uncertified ones. Such certification would prove to be extremely useful in the process of reputation building, essential to any payment instrument supplier, and could contribute in avoiding crisis of confidence.

To conclude, Internet payment instruments will significantly affect Central Bank operating procedures. For the moment, there are no risks of systemic instability, but as these new instruments take off Central Banks will have to adapt their behaviour to take them into account, to avoid that certain behaviours become customs. Such changes will have to take place early enough to avoid that some crisis of one operator gives rise to an overall crisis of confidence in Internet payments.

7

Internet Banking: A New Paradigm

Deepak Kumar, Shashi Kapoor and Neelam Khullar

7.1 Introduction

The core issues faced by banks today are on the fronts of customer's service expectations, cutting operational costs and managing competition. For this, banks are exploring new financial products and services options that would help them to grow without losing existing customers. And any new financial product or service that a bank offers will be intrinsically related to technology. Only technology can help banks in meeting these objectives. That's why Information Technology has just moved from being a business enabler to being a business driver.

Modern banking is no longer confined to the branches only. Now day's Indian customers are being provided with multiple modes of accessing banking transactions, including Tele-banking, Mobile banking, Internet banking, PC banking and Banking through ATMs. Internet banking is one of the latest arrays in India. It has the core features and functions designed to improve the customer retention and adoption while placing the utmost emphasis on system security. From simple account review to sophisticated payment transfer and self-service functionality, Internet banking provides the online experience that distinguishes our financial institutions from their competitors.

Internet banking enables a customer to do banking transactions through the bank's website on the Internet. It is a system of accessing accounts and general information on bank products and services through a computer while sitting in its office or home. This is also called virtual banking. It is more or less bringing the bank to you computer. In traditional banking one has to approach the branch in person, to withdraw cash or deposit a cheque or request a statement of accounts etc. but Internet banking has changed the way of banking. Now one can operate all these types of transaction on his computer through website of bank. All such transactions are encrypted, using sophisticated multi-layered security architecture, including firewalls and filters. One can be rest assured that one's transactions are secure and confidential.

7.2 Online Banking, PC Banking and Internet Banking

Internet Banking is different from online banking and PC banking. Online banking is a wider term which includes Internet banking, Phone banking, Mobile banking, banking through ATM and PC banking etc. On the other hand, PC banking is making transactions through a PC at one's home or office, which is connected to a particular branch through Modem. PC banking is available when that branch is open and is available through that particular PC only. But Internet banking enables to do the same through any PC connected to the Internet, at any time and from anywhere in the world.

7.2.1 Types of Internet Banking: Currently, there are three basic kinds of Internet banking that are being employed in the marketplace:

A. Information: This is the most basic level of Internet banking. The bank has marketing information about its products and services on a stand-alone server. This level of Internet banking service can be provided by the bank itself or by sourcing it out. Since the server or Web site may be vulnerable to alteration, appropriate controls must therefore be in place to prevent unauthorized alterations to data in the server or web site.

B. Communication: This type of Internet banking allows interaction between the bank's systems and the customer. It may be limited to electronic mail, account inquiry, loan applications, or static file updates. The risk is higher with this configuration than with the earlier system and therefore appropriate controls need to be in place to prevent, monitor, and-alert management of any unauthorized attempt to access bank's internal network and computer systems. Under this system the client makes a request to which the bank subsequently responds.

C. Transaction: Under this system of Internet banking customers are allowed to execute transactions. Relative to the information and communication types of Internet banking, this system possesses the highest level of risk architecture and must have the strongest controls. Customer transactions can include accessing accounts, paying bills, transferring funds, etc. These possibilities demand very stringent security.

7.2.2 Types of Services Available: Through Internet banking, customers can not only get account balance and see statements of account online but they can also transfer funds, order demand drafts, pay utility bills etc. Following types of main transactions or operations can be performed through Internet banking:

Basic

- Account Information
- Funds Transfer
- Bill Presentment and Payment

Premium

- On line Payment for Shopping done on Internet
- Loan Applications
- Standing Instructions
- Request and Intimations
- Financial Advice
- Credit and Debit Cards
- Investment Transactions
- Customer Correspondence
- Opening Accounts
- Insurance
- Other Value Added /Premium Services etc.

7.2.3 Growth of Internet Banking: The growth of Internet banking business has been very encouraging and consequently financial institutions are actively promoting Internet banking.

Internet banking has grown up all over the world is evident from Table 7.1.

Table 7.1: Number of Customers Using Internet Banking

(million)

	2000	2001	2002	2003	2004
Asia Pacific (including India but excluding Japan)	2.4	4.4	6.8	9.8	13.8
Japan	2.5	6.5	11.9	19.6	21.8
United States	9.9	14.7	17.1	20.4	22.8
Western Europe	18.6	28.0	37.8	47.7	57.9
Rest of the World	1.0	1.7	3.1	5.1	6.1

Source: International Data Corporation, epaynews.com

From the above table, we can analyze that number of Internet Banking Customers are increasing manifold from 34.4 million in 2000 to 122.4 million in 2004 showing a growth of more than 350 per cent in just 4 years all over world. Moreover, numbers of customers banking online is expected to increase significantly over the next few years and that too not merely in the industrial nations but also in the developing countries like India.

7.3 Factors Responsible for Growth of Internet Banking

Numerous factors including competitive cost, customer service, and demographic considerations are motivating banks to evaluate their technology and assess their Internet banking strategies. The challenge for national banks is to make sure the savings from Internet banking technology more than offset the costs and risks associated with conducting business in cyberspace. Marketing strategies will vary as national banks seek to expand their markets and employ lower cost delivery channels. Examiners will need to understand the strategies used and technologies employed on a bank-by-bank basis to assess the risk. Evaluating a bank's data on the use of their Web sites, may help examiners determine the bank's strategic objectives, how well the bank is meeting its Internet banking product plan, and whether the business is expected to be profitable.

7.3.1 Competition: Studies show that competitive pressure is the chief driving force behind increasing use of Internet banking technology, ranking ahead of cost reduction and revenue enhancement, in second and third place respectively. Banks see Internet banking as a way to keep existing customers and attract new ones to the bank.

7.3.2 Cost Efficiencies: Banks can deliver banking services on the Internet at transaction costs far lower than traditional brick-and-mortar branches. The actual costs to execute a transaction will vary depending on the delivery channel used. The frequently quoted Booz-Allen and Hamilton study showed that the cost of a customer walking into the branch and using a teller is US$1.01, where as the cost of conducting the same transaction on the Internet is only a tenth of the cost. No doubt the ATM is considerably cheaper than a teller, but even so, the Internet is nearly 3 times cheaper than the ATM usage. In short, replacing a teller with an Internet channel should in theory, show a 10 fold increase in the distribution revenue for the bank. This reason alone should be sufficient for banks to encourage this form of distribution channel.

However, banks should use care in making product decisions. Management should include in their decision making the development and ongoing costs associated with a new product or service, including the technology, marketing, maintenance, and customer support functions. This will help management exercise due diligence, make more informed decisions, and measure the success of their business venture.

7.3.3 Geographical Reach: Internet banking allows expanded customer contact through increased geographical reach and lower cost delivery channels. In fact some banks are doing business exclusively via the Internet. They do not have traditional banking offices and only reach their customers online. Other financial institutions are using the Internet as an alternative delivery channel to reach existing customers and attract new customers.

7.3.4 Branding: Relationship building is a strategic priority for many national banks. Internet banking technology and products can provide a means for national banks to develop and maintain an ongoing relationship with their customers by offering easy access to a broad array of products and services. By capitalizing on brand identification and by providing a broad array of financial services, banks hope to build customer loyalty, cross-sell, and enhance repeat business.

7.3.5 Customer Demographics: Internet banking allows national banks to offer a wide array of options to their banking customers. Some customers will rely on traditional branches to conduct their banking business. For many, this is the most comfortable way for them to transact their banking business. Those customers place a premium on person-to-person contact. Other customers are early adopters of new technologies that arrive in the marketplace. These customers were the first to obtain PCs and the first to employ them in conducting their banking business. The demographics of banking customers will continue to change. The challenge to national banks is to understand their customer base and find the right mix of delivery channels to deliver products and services profitably to their various market segments.

7.3.6 Round the Clock Access: Internet banking services are available on 24x7 basis to the customers without charging any extra cost from the customers. And one can access the bank from any where in the world at one's own convenience without owning your own PC.

7.4 Internet Banking: Risk Factors

If Internet banking has facilitated the banking service processes and made the customers life a lot easier, it has also thrown new challenges in terms of various risks which may affect the banks profitability, capital and reputation as well. Let us discuss some of the risk issues related to the online banking.

7.4.1 Operational Risk: Operational risk is the price, which attaches to Internet banking arising from error, fraud, and inability to provide services to customers or deliver products as per the expectation, which may result in current and prospective loss to earnings of the bank. Inaccurate processing of transactions, non enforceability of contracts, compromises in data integrity, data privacy and confidentiality, attacks or unauthorized access to banks systems and databases, weak technology adoption or systems design or human factors like lack of awareness on the part of employees or customers may lead to operational risk.

7.4.2 Credit Risk: Credit risk arises when a counter-party fails to settle an obligation when due or any time henceforth for its full value. In Internet banking scenario the credit worthiness of the customer may not be properly evaluated. So any credit facilities provided to retail or corporate customers requires proper evaluation and constant audit of lending as well as the repayment progress at regular intervals to avoid such a risk.

7.4.3 Liquidity Risk: The bank may face liquidity crunch in short-term time horizon in Internet banking scenario as well. In this case, the outflow of fund may be sudden and hence the banks, which are more exposed to Internet banking, should ensure for sufficient liquidity in case of redemption or settlement demands.

7.4.4 Foreign Exchange Risk: Due to the geographical and market extension of banks and customers in Internet banking scenario forex, legal and regulatory risk may arise. In cross border transactions there would be difficulty in correctly assessing the counter-parties credentials and hence forex transaction against electronic money may lead to forex risk. Different international cross-border jurisdiction can expose banks to legal and compliance risks in view of different national rules, laws and regulations.

7.4.5 Security Risk: Security risk is one of very important issue in Internet banking systems. In Internet banking information is considered as an asset and so worthy of protection. Firewalls are frequently used on Internet banking systems as security measure to protect internal systems and should be considered for any system connected to an outside network. Firewalls are a combination of hardware and software placed between two networks through which all traffic must pass, regardless of direction flow. They provide gateway to guard against unauthorized individuals gaining access to the bank's network. Therefore, awareness among the Internet banking customers as well as adoption of security mechanism is essential.

7.4.6 Compliance Risk: The bank may face compliance and regulatory risk if it does not adhere or follow the guidelines given by the supervisor or the regulator. Due to lack of awareness and transparency the bank may fail in this matter and hence more care is required in this area.

7.4.7 Reputation Risk: A bank offering internet banking suffers reputation loss due to negative opinion if the systems failed or discontinued for a considerable time or when the banking products offered not found to their expectations or even the fraudulent activities by the internal / external people or hackers using bona fide customer's credentials. The bank-customer relationship may suffer due to this and this may also affect bringing prospective customers to its fold.

7.4.8 Legal Risk: Internet banking being a relatively a new phenomenon, the legal issues or risks are usually less crystallized or ambiguous. They may arise from violation of, or non-conformance with laws, rules, regulations, or prescribed practices. Due to uncertainty about the validity of some agreements formed via electronic media and law regarding customer disclosures and privacy protection, legal risks may arise. A bank may also face legal actions from the customers in case of hushing attacks or any other fraudulent activities where the terms and conditions have not been framed adequately by the bank. If a bank does not ensure proper security mechanism of its system, it opens itself for legal action.

7.4.9 Strategic Risk: Strategic risk may emanate from adverse business decisions due to wrong implementation or unfavorable market conditions related to either the banking products offered through electronic channel, or any technology or strategic decisions like outsourcing policy, technology policy, etc. Therefore, a proper market as well as technological survey is essential in this regard before taking any final decision.

7.4.10 Money Laundering Risk: In view of the lack of personal interaction among the bank staff and the customers in the internet banking scenario, the Know Your Customers (KYC) norms may not be implemented effectively as fund transfer transactions of dubious nature may be done by the offenders without much of hassles. Money laundering activities in smaller chunks over a time-period may be carried out through internet banking.

7.4.11 Interest Rate Risk: In case of electronic money becoming widely prevalent in the payment system, the interest rate risk and market risk will have an impact on the value of the banks assets against its electronic money liabilities.

7.5 Internet Banking: Indian Scenario

In India, Slowly but steadily, the Indian customer is moving towards Internet Baking. A number of banks have either adopted Internet Banking or are on the threshold of adopting it. The Banks started Internet Banking initially with simple function such as getting information about interest rates, checking account balances and computing loan eligibility. Then the services were extended to online bill payment, transfer of funds between accounts and cash management services for corporate. Recently banks have started to facilitate payment for e-commerce transactions by directly debiting bank accounts or through credit cards. It will add to the revenues of the banks.

Malhotra and Singh (2005) studied the current state of Internet Banking services offered by the private, public and foreign banks operating in India (Tables 7.2 and 7.3). Almost, all the banks are having websites, however only 33 banks are providing transactional banking services in one form or the other.

However, Out of 33 banks providing internet banking, only 16 banks provide Internet banking in true sense.

Table 7.2: Internet Banking in India

(As on March 31, 2005)

	Number of Banks	Number of Banks with Websites	Number of Banks Providing Internet Banking
Private Sector Banks	29	26	13
Public Sector Banks	27	27	15
Foreign Banks	33	32	5
All Banks	89	85	33

Table 7.3: Classification of Internet Banking Websites

(As on March 31, 2005)

	Entry Level	Transactional Websites		Total Number of Bank websites
		Partly Transactional	Fully Transactional*	
All Banks	52	17	16	85
Public Sector Banks	12	11	4	27
Private Sector Banks	13	5	8	26
Foreign Banks	27	1	4	32

*Fully transactional Internet banks include those banks providing Basic plus premium services of Internet Banking.

It was ICICI Bank, which initiated the electronic banking revolution in India when they introduced Internet banking as early as 1997 under the Brand name 'Infinity'. This was soon followed by HDFC in Sept.1999, IndusInd, Global Trust Bank etc. However, of late many public sector banks and scheduled commercial banks like SBI, BOI, BOB, Syndicate Bank, Allahabad Bank, PNB etc. to name a few have taken a lead in this area. As estimated 4.6 million Indian Internet users are banking through Internet. This figure is expected to reach around 16 million by 2007-08.

7.6 Internet Banking: Issues

The main issues in Internet banking today relate to security, authentication, non-repudiation, privacy, trust, internet banking business continuance plan, security awareness and security breach detection and reporting etc.; they are not only relevant for the banks but for the satisfaction and confidence of the customers. The objective must be to provide a robust and reliable technological platform, which ensures authentication, non-repudiation, availability of services, integrity and confidentiality of data and transaction, trust and privacy.

- **Security:** In Internet banking information is considered as an asset and so worthy of protection. Security concerns in the Internet scenario manifest in the use of public network and related security threats online. The bank should put in place proper and tested IT infrastructure and software.
- **Authentication:** User authentication assumes a great significance in Internet banking as customers log on to the system from different locations without any physical means of authentication. Therefore, proper identification and authentication procedures should be established and followed to establish accountability and to prevent unauthorized persons from gaining access to the systems. This can be achieved through, for example, passwords or smart tokens; logical access controls to establish who has access to a specific type of information resources and the type of access permitted.
- **Non-Repudiation:** The non-repudiation issue is one of the most important issues in online banking. No customer should later claim that any particular transaction was not transacted by him / her. Thus, proper authentication and authorization mechanism using encryption and digital signature should be established.

- **Privacy:** The bank should provide privacy of the data and the transaction in all circumstances except in cases when instructed by the competent legal authority or the government to divulge the same. Even if the website or database maintenance is outsourced, the bank should take the primary responsibility of preventing breach of confidentiality. Thus, privacy not only covers confidentiality of the banks data but also guarantees the data's level of privacy, which is being used by different operators at different levels of authorization.
- **Availability:** The Internet banking services should be available round-the-clock to the customers or else the goodwill and reputation of the bank will take a beating resulting in financial loss as well as losing out loyal customers. The system should be up and running in reliable manner when needed and timely access to resources should be ensured all the time.
- **System Architecture and Design:** The choice of technological infrastructure generally determines the success of Internet banking in the long run. A correct system architecture and design will help in managing operational and security risks to a greater extent. The banking services can also be catered in a reliable fashion. The bank should take care that any financial transaction should move only in a secure environment.
- **Trust:** In Internet banking establishment of trust among the parties is essential. This can be established through a trusted third party designated as a Certification Authority (CA). The digital certificates issued by the CA to various entities along with at least two factor identification mechanisms can be trusted for the authentication and non-repudiation of the users and the transactions in internet banking.
- **Business Continuity Planning:** The business continuity planning should be an integral part of banks internet banking policy. It ensures that the bank can prevent interruptions, and recover and resume processing in the event of a partial or complete interruption internet banking system/services

availability. A long delay in making available the services to the customers in case of disruption of the internet banking system may erode the banks credibility and goodwill as well as the customers' confidence in the banks internet banking services.

- **Security awareness, training, and education:** The purpose of creating awareness towards information security in the area of Internet banking through training and education is necessary for understanding the need of information security, protection of passwords, awareness about various spywares and malicious codes. Advanced training for the system administrators may also be conducted to optimally configure the Internet banking system and update them about the latest threats being present in the Internet banking domain.
- **Security breach detection and Incidence Response System:** One major area of concern today in Internet banking is the timely detection of security breach and incident response mechanism to perform the necessary damage control exercise. Follow up and exception reporting of logs like audit log, systems log, users log, etc. become important tasks. Responsibilities and accountability of the key personnel along with other staff members should be clearly demarcated.

7.7 Conclusion

The banking industry is now a very mature one and banks are being forced to change rapidly as a result of open market forces such as threat of competition, customer demand, and technological innovations such as growth of Internet banking. If banks have to retain their competitiveness, they must focus on customer retention and relationship management, upgrade and offer integration and value added services. With the increasing customer demands, banks have to constantly think of innovative customized services to remain competitive. That's why Internet banking is becoming a necessity today.

Popularity which Internet banking has won among customers, owing to its speed, convenience and round-the-clock access they offer, is likely to increase in the future. That's why Internet banking is a successful strategic weapon for banks to remain profitable in volatile and competitive marketplace of today. Banks are in a position to lead consumer views, as well as to cater to existing demands. Clearly, despites of all the threats in banking industry, there is an enormous opportunity for farsighted banks to reap the rewards available from Internet banking. Internet banking is going to develop much faster than most people imagine. And with the revolution, a new financial system will evolve that in many ways will be far more secure than the one we have today.

References

Booz-Allen & Hamitton (2003), Processing Cost Per Transaction, *JP Morgans*

Comptroller's handbook (1999), Internet Banking, *Comptroller of the Currency Administrator of National Banks*, October.

Harman, S (2001), The future of the Internet Banking, *Smart Investor*, Issue 132, April.

International Data Cooperation, 'Growth in Internet Banking', available at www.epaynews.com

K Arvind, Surjit, 'Internet Banking: Concepts, Risks and Issues', available at www.rbi.org.in

Malhotra, Pooja and Singh, Balwinder (2005), New Revolution in the Indian Banking Industry, *Punjab Journal of Business Studies*, April-Sept., Vol.1, No.1.

Mishra A. K. 'Internet Banking in India' available at www.banknetindia.com

Narayana V. (2000), Nuts and Bolts of Internet Banking, *Investment World*, July 16.

Patrick R Anil (2003), The Tech Factor in Banking-Technology in Banking, *Network Magazine*, May.

Perumel, Vignesen & Shanmugam, Bala, 'Internet Banking: Boon or Bane?' Available at www.arreydev.com

Singhal, S (2003), Internet Banking-The second wave, *Banker's guide to Internet Strategy in the Post Dotcom Era*, Tata McGraw-Hill Publications.

Unnithan, C.R. and Swatman, P. (2001), E-banking Adaptation and Dot.com Viability-A Comparison of Australian and Indian

Experiences in the Banking Sector, Working Paper, School of management Information Systems, Deakin University, No.14

8

Economics of ATM

Leena Kakkar

8.1 Introduction

The Automated Teller Machine (ATM) is seen everywhere. This machine has brought Innovations in the Banking sector all over the world. The advent of the ATM has made the concept of round the clock banking a reality. The ATM has been helpful to both the bankers and the customers. The long crowd of customers in the banking hall of a branch waiting for their turn to collect cash is disappearing. The branch business timings have lost significance to the customers after the introduction of ATM.

The ATM is a device used by the bank customers to process account transactions. The customer inserts into the ATM, a plastic card i.e. encoded with information on a magnetic strip. The strip contains an identification code that is transmitted to the bank's central computer by modem. Every cardholder should be given a PIN (personal identification number) that he should enter and after verifying the same with the records, ATM would allow operations.

8.2 Functions of ATM

The functions of ATM differ from Bank to Bank. The following features are available in the ATM of all the Banks.

- Fast cash: when you want to do the only activity of drawing cash in pre-determined amounts like Rs. 500, Rs. 1,000, Rs. 2,000, Rs. 5,000 etc. you can use this option.
- Normal cash withdrawal: Every bank has fixed a maximum limit of cash withdrawal per account per day. It ranges between Rs. 10-15000. While in some banks the maximum amount may be drawn in one shot (HDFC, ICICI) and in

some other banks it should be drawn in lots (Syndicate Bank, State Bank of India). All withdrawals shall be in multiple of Rs.100 only.

- Balance Enquiry
- Mini statement of account: You get detail of last 5–10 transactions.
- PIN change:
- Cash Deposit: Varied procedures exist. Here special covers are available in the ATM wherein the client has to fill up the challan, the denominations and key in these details. Then, a window opens wherein the cover containing the cash has to be dropped. At the end of the day, officials of the branch to which the ATM is attached, would open the machine, take the cover and credit the account of the customer. If there is any difference between the amount fed and the actual cash in the cover, the decision of the bank is final.
- Transfer transactions: If you want to transfer funds with in the bank i.e. from one account to another at same branch or at different branch, you can use this option.

8.3 Economics of ATM

The cost of ATM has drastically come down over the past 5 years. From an average original investment of Rs. 15 lakh, it has been reduced to Rs. 9 lakh. In addition a recurring cost of Rs. 1 lakh per month has to be incurred. With this cost pattern, around 180 transactions per day are required to break even.

The cost of each transaction at the branch of the Bank is Rs. 60 while it is Rs. 10 if carried out through ATM. Nearly 93 per cent of UTI Bank's retail cash transactions are done through its ATM's. This is the highest compared to other Bank's like ICICI Bank and HDFC bank.

8.4 Advantages of ATM

To Banks

- Less space required
- Capital expenditure is lower as compared to Branch

- Bank's staff gets more time to do marketing
- Lower transaction cost
- One more means for advertising Bank's Products

To Customers

- Convenience of shopping- no need to carry cash
- No need to visit branch for transaction
- AAA Banking-Any time, Anywhere, Anyhow.
- Fast and efficient service
- Good currency notes

8.5 Do's and Do Not's for ATM Users

Do's

- Keep your card in your purse/wallet where it won't get scratched
- Get your card after you enter the ATM cubicle
- Make your PIN series of letters or numbers that you can easily remember but that cannot be easily be associated with you personally.
- After your transaction, take your receipt, card and money away.
- Position your hand and body in such a way that the PIN entry cannot be recorded by camera.
- If you find that cash received from ATM is short, complain to the security, if there is one or else phone up your branch and inform immediately so that they would look into your grievance.
- If some one picks your pocket and you loose the card as well, inform the card issuing Bank immediately and also file an FIR with the nearest police station.
- Check your monthly statement to make certain all charges are your own and immediately notify the card issuer of any error or unauthorized changes.

Do Not's

- Do not write your PIN. If you still feel it necessary, do not keep this along with the wallet in which the card is kept.

- Avoid using birth dates, initials, house number, phone number as PIN.
- Do not reveal your PIN to any one, including close friends because that is the security failure on which the entire ATM works.
- Do not through the receipt in and around ATM area. It is suggested that you destroy it by tearing into pieces since it contains your account no: and card no: which might be misused.

8.6 Types of Plastic Money

- **ATM Card:** This card would be useful only to operate the ATM.
- **Debit Card:** This Card would be useful to make payments for purchase from member establishments who have arrangements with the card issuing bank/agency. All Card issuers are affiliated to two major issuers- VISA and Master Card. This is a Card similar to Credit Card.
- **Debit-cum-ATM Card:** This is the most common these days. The same Debit Card can be used to draw cash from ATM and also make payments to shops for purchases. This is Two-in- one Card.
- **Credit Card:** This Card enable the client to obtain goods or services from various shops having arrangements with the issuing agency even when there is no balance in his savings or current account. Normally a limit would be fixed based on the net worth of the client up to which the client can use the Card. The same card can be used even to draw cash from ATM'S with in the cash limit approved to that client. Normally, at the time of issuing the Card, The Bank would intimate the client two limits (spending limits) - one the total spending limit (based on the net worth of the client) and the other sub limit with in the total spending limit for the purpose of drawing cash, e.g. a Card may have a total spending limit of Rs. 1 lakh with a sub limit for cash withdrawal of Rs. 20,000.

- The functions performed by Debit and Credit Cards are same. The only difference is that in case of Debit Cards the transactions can be put through if and only if balance is available in customers account but in Credit Cards even without balance in the account the client can operate-subject of course to the maximum limit fixed.
- Credit Cards are normally valid in the country of issue. For example, the Credit Card issued by Banks in India, would be valid through out India. If the Bank has arrangement with agencies in foreign countries, it may issue a Credit Card to selected clients, which would be valid abroad as well. Such Cards are termed as International Credit Card.
- **Charge Card:** A Charge Card is similar to a Credit Card with one major difference, with a Charge Card you have to pay the entire dues with in the credit period and cannot carry over any balance like Credit Card.
- **Co-Branded Cards:** Some times Banks that issues Cards enter into agreement with other entities (air lines, hotels) etc. So that both are in a win-win situation i.e. the no: of Cards of the issuing Bank increase by which their fee based income would go up and the sales of the Co-branded Company's product would also increase.

  Co-Branded Cards, which are affiliated with merchants such as airlines and retailers, use rewards programmes and special offers including rebates, discounts and gifts certificates to attract new customers, generate loyalty among existing customers and ultimately increase Card usages. The future of Co-Branded Cards across all industries seems bright.

8.7 Future of ATM

Although ATM machines were originally developed as cash dispensers, they have evolved to include many other Bank related functions. In future, ATM may perform functions that are not directly related to mgt of one's own Bank account such as paying routine bills, fees and taxes.

ATM's have a great role to play in India. All Banks have come together through an arrangement by which each Banks customer can access the ATM of other member Banks without any extra cost. This would ensure lower cost to the Bank and higher and efficient utilization of already installed ATM's. The National Financial Switch (NFS) network, which is aimed and maintained by the Institute for Development and Research in Banking Technology is the technical aim of the RBI and aims at linking all ATM's in the country for providing efficient and cheaper ATM operations. Many public and private sector Bank's are becoming members of NFS to get the benefit of over 9000 ATM's.

Efforts are on to manufacture ATM's that would be supplied around Rs 2 lakh. This would help in taking the ATM to the rural areas of the country to suit the rural people and also as an additional security device innovations are being made in the form of using camera inside the ATM, which would picture the client and compare with the records or use thumb impressions of the client for identification etc.

Thus the ATM's would be the 'Banking of the future' and the brick and mortar branches would slowly disappear. Both Banker and the clients, due to its various benefits have adapted themselves to the ATM culture.

9

Is Web Business Good Business?

Rimpi Jatana, Nittu Gupta and R.K. Uppal

Although tangible returns are elusive, the first wave of W based companies have learned valuable lessons about how make the most out of a presence on the Net.

When wine buyer Peter Granoff was looking for a way ou the restaurant business, he never dreamed his future lay cyberspace. Then one evening over dinner as his brother-in- Robert Olson sketched out a plan for a starting a company on World Wide Web, Granoff had a vision. Olson, a for marketing executive at a Silicon Valley computer maker, war to sell an easy-to-distribute product with a large, passionate, geographically dispersed buying audience. He believed the id product line for the Web was one whose customers nee extensive information to guide their purchasing decisions. excited Granoff said, "You're talking about my busine Inspired, Granoff and Olson launched Virtual Vineyards, a rapi growing online vendor of wine and one of the first of a grow number of companies that are illustrating the revenue-generat potential of putting a storefront on the World Wide Web.

Companies that continue to do most of their sales thro conventional channels are setting up Web sites as promotional a corporate image tools. At the same time, the Net has given birth a rising number of Web-only enterprises.

It costs little to set up a rudimentary Web site that provic information on a company's products and services. And foreca of the Web's business potential can be tantalizing. One often-ci source, Matrix Information Directory Services, predicts that number of people online will expand from 57 million in 1997 377 million in 2000. According to a Nielson Media Resear eport, 2.5 million persons already have bought products or ervices on the Web. And Forrester Research, a market-research irm in Cambridge, Mass., predicts that Internet-based sales in the Jnited States will jump from $ 518 million this year to $ 6,600 nillion by decade's end. Over the same period, Jupiter Communications, a New York firm that studies online and nteractive technologies, projects that Web advertising will xpand from $ 312 million to $ 5,000 million.

Internet businesses have found that cybershoppers are attracted by the ability to research and compare products before nitiating transactions-in contrast to the world of brick-and-mortar commerce, where customers often rush into purchases or must ravel from store to store to compare products effectively. Web sites can offer more detailed and extensive information than a ypical customer-service representative is willing or able to provide, either in person or over the telephone. The Internet marketplace also may be well-suited for customers looking for are or hard-to-find items. Mike Schachner, managing editor of Wine Enthusiast magazine, predicts that a Web-based outfit like Virtual Vineyards will do especially well selling specialty or high-priced wines, as opposed to the "$ 10 bottle of Cabernet to have with your steak" that consumers will still buy from local shops on the way home from work.

But making money on the Web is hardly a slam-dunk. Most early online retail ventures have failed to generate enough sales to survive, and a 1996 survey of online businesses by the market-research firm ActivMedia found that just under one-third of Internet-based firms claim to be profitable. Many consumers are unwilling to change established buying patterns, or are repelled by clumsy attempts at online marketing; people are reluctant to type their credit card number onto a Web site for fear that it will be stolen.

Right now, most companies are trying to establish themselves as major presences online and playing the game of increasing their name recognition and market share. The payoff, these companies believe, will come down the road in a year or so, when

Web commerce becomes more commonplace. For example, Darryl Peck, founder of Cyberian Outpost, an online computer retailer, says his company posts $ 2 million in monthly sales, attracts 12,000 visitors a day, and has recorded an annual growth rate of 600 percent over the last two years. Ask about profit and loss, though, and the picture isn't so rosy. The investment in hardware, network access, and people to make a Web site efficient and attractive is substantial. Says Peck, "Our loss was under 9 per cent of sales last year. That puts us a lot closer to profitability than most Web companies." At this embryonic stage of the Web marketplace, Peck maintains, strong revenue, steady growth, and high volume of traffic at the Web site, rather than net profit - are a better guide to a Web-based business's success.

Virtual Vineyards founder Granoff says that his company is growing at an average of 20 per cent per month and that its "trend lines are all in the right direction." Preview Travel, which provides online travel and vacation planning information through America Online and its own Web site, claims to have 1.4 million subscribers, weekly bookings of between $ 1.2 million and $ 1.6 million, and a growth rate of about 20 percent per month. Hot & Spicy Foods of Morgan Hill, Calif., opened a Web site in November and saw an immediate spurt in business; sales during the first quarter of this year were double what they were during the same period of 1996, according to President Jeffrey Marcil. These and other successful sites emphasize transaction efficiency, rapid response, and tools for customizing the customer's visit. They frequently allow visitors to make contributions to the site or talk with each other in a way that makes them feel like members of a community.

SET is working today in limited pilot tests, which are controlled These cybermerchants are learning that even in a medium as exotic as the Web, all the rules of traditional business still apply. Companies need to get strong financial backing, find customers, offer high-quality products, process orders efficiently, and win repeat sales. But to survive the early shakeout period, Web-based enterprises must also do more than simply master these fundamentals of Marketing. Merchants need imagination to design shopping environments tailored to the Web's unique strengths and weaknesses.

Judging from the business climate on the Web, many companies have made rapid progress toward learning the craft of Internet marketing. Online retailers provide entertaining and informative sites that customize shopping for the individual consumer and even anticipate consumers' buying preferences. Despite such developments, the financial prospects of Internet commerce are hard to gauge. Information that has been released focuses on the cheeriest statistics the companies can muster, such as the number of visitors to their online stores and the rate of revenue growth. While this is an appropriate mentality for a start-up business, it can carry a company only so far. Eventually, costs must be covered. And as the novelty of the Web wears off, the challenge of offering a distinct and customer-friendly site becomes ever tougher- and more essential.

9.1 Tapping the Wonders of Web

Many early-adapting businesses have struggled with how best to use the new medium. Commonly, companies fail to exploit the capacity for interactivity, offering static sites that serve as electronic versions of brochures. Successful companies, in contrast, have developed dynamic, information-rich sites that create an informal, often whimsical atmosphere that consumers enjoy searching whether they buy products or not, and that take advantage of the Internet's unique attributes. Good Web business sites offer visitors a wealth of useful, diverting information in addition to detailed product descriptions. Virtual Vineyards, for instance, publishes a "tasting chart" that helps shoppers learn how to judge wines by intensity, sweetness, body, acidity, tannin oak, and complexity. It also provides a glossary of frequently used terms and tips on how to mix wine and food and an archive of menus, including recipes and wine choices, for a variety of holidays and special occasions.

Online booksellers are also employing innovative ways to use free information to stimulate sales. Amazon.com devotes a Web page to each book that the cyberstore sells, and many of the more popular offerings feature links to author interviews and reviews by professional critics. Another Internet bookstore, PureFiction in England, not only reprints snippets of critical reactions to its featured offerings but also publishes sample chapters and offers five-minute audio excerpts of its books on tape.

Early-adapting companies have found that too much visual sophistication can be counterproductive. Frustrated shoppers ball out of business Web sites quickly when detailed renderings of products or other images take too long to load on their computer screens. ReadMe.Doc, a computer-book retailer in Chambersburg, Pa., recently scaled back on the number of graphic images on its site because "It was taking too long for someone with a 14.4-kilobit-per-second modem to get a page up," says President Christopher Kendall.

In a similar vein, Perry Lopez, creator of Hot Hot Hot, a hot-sauce retailer in Los Angeles, stresses the importance of easy navigation. He has tried to create a Web site where customers have to click only once from the home page to get to key information in any given category. But such an approach is a matter of personal taste; some Web users prefer pages with small amounts of information and frequent links.

Internet business experts caution would-be cybermarketers that good Web site design takes time. It is deceptively easy to throw together a quick-and-dirty Web page in a few hours. But a high-quality site that customers will feel comfortable visiting and revisiting requires planning and maintenance. Successful electronic merchants make detailed studies of commercial Web sites before designing or opening an electronic business. For instance, Darryl Peck says he "spent 16 hours a day checking out Web sites" before formulating a business plan for Cyberian Outpost. Similarly, the founders of Amazon.com spent a year learning the business before going online, according to Scott Lipsky, vice president of business expansion.

Web business veterans recommend bringing in outsiders or customers to evaluate a new site before launch. AMP, one of the world's leading manufacturers of electronic and electrical connectors, took a year to develop a Web site allowing online parts purchase. For almost six months before the site officially opened, major customers piloted the new system and offered comments on its usability, according to Robert Orendorf, project manager for AMP eMerce Internet Solutions. And Virtual Vineyards took nine months to develop a product inventory system to support the company's Web site, accommodating more than 75 wineries and 45 specially-food companies.

9.2 Attracting and Keeping Customers

There is nothing so forlorn as an unvisited Web site. Companies that want to attract people to their online storefront use a variety of channels, both on and off the Internet, to attract potential customers. One approach is to send marketing offers to customers through electronic mail. Such efforts need not be the kind of unsolicited junk mail, or "spam," that so enrages many recipients. Many Web sites ask visitors to register, a process that offers the option of signing up for e-mail from the company announcing product news.

One technique that universally attracts customers to a Web site is visualizations of products. When engineers search the AMP Connect Web catalog, for example, they can navigate among 70,000 choices by part name or number, or by using a menu of product pictures. Once customers have found products meeting their specifications, they can view detailed line drawings, and in some cases, download three-dimensional renderings. At Toyota's Web site, customers can not only read text screens with detailed product specifications and dealer locations but can see what a variety of colors look like on a car model, view new automobiles from different vantage points through photographic "walkarounds," and look at interiors through a special "photobubble" view like that provided by a fisheye lens.

Granted, such attempts to visualize cars are primitive compared with what consumers see when visiting an automobile dealership. And shoppers often have to go through an involved process of downloading free software to use such effects. But car buying on the Web has proven surprisingly popular, especially in the form of online brokering services that gather product information and handle transactions. The Auto-By-Tel site, for example, provides access to financing and insurance information as well as an electronic form for requesting no-haggle, no-obligation price quotes on specific car models. Since starting up in 1995, the company has processed 325,000 requests for quotes from a network of 1,500 accredited dealerships.

In the San Francisco Bay area, the 12-dealership Tasha Automotive Group has sold several hundred cars through another Web-based buying service, Autoreach, according to Jon Fisher, director of operations. Although those represent less than 5 percent of total sales, Fisher expects more than 20 percent of his company's sales to come from the Internet within five years, based on recent growth trends. Fisher is particularly excited about the potential of Web sites to alleviate consumer disgust with the high-pressure sales and marketing tactics common in the automotive business.

9.3 Building Electronic Communities

Surfing the World Wide Web can be an adventure, but online users are often eager to relieve the loneliness of the ride. Many Internet businesses are trying to tap into the desire for interpersonal connection by establishing hospitable sites. People need to feel that someone is listening and responding on the other end of the modem.

While fast and consistent response is a basic of good business in any case, entrepreneurs have found its importance magnified on the Web. Shoppers want some confirmation other than a message box on a Web site that their orders have been processed. The rapidity of e-mail transmission has accustomed Internet users to expect responses to their questions and concerns within hours instead of days. Scott Lipsky of Amazon.com says that the company strives to answer every e-mail note-usually within hours. With the site's business growing by 30 percent each month, this task has become more daunting with each passing week, and the bookseller has continually beefed up its staff to meet this demand.

Business Web sites also gain by fostering a sense of community among their visitors. The first prerequisite of community-building is to offer a place "where people want to hang out," says Lee McKnight, a specialist in Internet economics and a lecturer in MIT's Technology, Management, and Policy Program. One way to do so is to address visitors in an informal, often humorous tone that encourages customers to have fun while making purchases or gathering product information. Visitors to Van den Bergh Foods' Ragu sauce site, for example, enter a cozy dining room dubbed "Mama's Cucina" where a grandmotherly woman waits at a table set for two. A dialogue bubble over her head says:

"You're buying a new computer? What's this new-new all the time now? I've got pots and pans older than you." In similarly colloquial language, Mama offers visitors recipes, Italian lessons, a free vacation contest, and advice on one's love life, along with information about Ragu products.

Some online businesses encourage a sense of community by allowing customers to contribute information to their sites. Virtual Vineyards publishes consumers' favorite ways to marry wine and food while offering the "Cork Dork" - a column that answers customer questions about wine. Amazon.com invites readers to post their comments about books it sells alongside those of professional critics.

Another tactic for building community is to emphasize interaction among customers. An excellent illustration of this approach is Onsale Inc., which conducts several virtual auctions a week of refurbished computers and home-electronics products. Shoppers can not only follow the progress of the auction and enjoy the pleasure of the hunt but can also include personal comments with their bids-and read those of other buyers. "They often get into competitive interactions, making comments like 'No way, MP of Mountain View, it's mine!!'" says marketing director Michelle Pettigrew. Onsale also stirs the pot by soliciting comments from bidders on topics not directly related to the purchase, posing questions such as "What's your favorite personal-computer game?" These interactions, says Pettigrew, help ensure that the auction is "not just a static online catalog or order-taking mechanism."

Onsale's strategy of combining entertainment with retailing appears to be paying off. The company says it has attained profitability with monthly sales exceeding $4 million. And according to PC Meter's recent audience rating reports for the World Wide Web, the online auction house often attracts visitors for more time each month than any other Internet shopping location. Between August 1996 and January 1997, Onsale shoppers spent an average of 30 to 48 minutes on the site each month.

Businesses gain further important advantages by maintaining strong electronic-mail contacts with customers. "A lot of times all you have to do is ask your customers for their opinions and feedback and you get a statistically reliable sample in a matter of hours," says Onsale's Pettigrew. "We use our customers as a sounding board whenever possible." Rosalind Resnick, president of a Web-site design company called NetCreations, considers the three hours a day she spends answering mail from customers as time well spent. "Customers are thrilled to get a response from the president of the company," she says, "The more interaction the better."

Indeed, Hot & Spicy Foods president Marcil says that what he likes best about adding an Internet component to his business is the rapid access it gives him to customers. He can make a change in product offerings and get the word out immediately to customers-both on his Web site and through targeted electronic mailings to regular cybershoppers at his store. The response rate to e-mail specials is around 5 to 7 per cent, he says, in contrast to the 3 to 4 per cent response elicited by traditional targeted mailings.

9.4 Customised Shopping

Successful online businesses have even found ways to tailor the shopping experience to individual buyers. These innovators give consumers tools that ease product searches or profile individuals' buying preferences and offer information tailored to their needs.

A good example is Preview Travel, where consumers have access to a powerful engine for customizing their trip plans. A would-be shopper enters a destination and preferred dates, times, and airline. An automated flight-planning system then displays a selection of flights that match the desired itinerary-including fare, seat availability, type of airplane, meals, number of stops, and the flight's on-time record.

Preview also offers best-fare options, reflecting the fact that the difference in cost for relatively small changes in plans can be significant. For instance, a recent request for a round-trip quote from Atlanta to Sydney, Australia, came in at slightly over $3,000 for the preferred times. The best-fare quote reduced that price nearly 50 percent by shifting the departure time for the Los Angeles-to-Sydney leg of the flight from late afternoon to early evening, and by changing the trip home from Sydney from around noon to mid-afternoon. While the same services are available from traditional travel agents, booking air tickets over the Web lets the consumer transact business at any hour of the day or night, and do comparative shopping.

Other Internet-based businesses are taking customization into a new dimension with software that digests information from consumers and then responds to their buying preferences. The Vertigo Group, for example, recently introduced One-on-One Banking Center software, which banks can make available for their customers to download from Web sites. The software leads consumers through an interview," eliciting basic personal information as well as details about their assets, debts, and investments. One-on-One then generates an "action plan" with recommendations for investing a specific amount of money in an equity mutual fund, opening a tax-deferred annuity at a given dollar level, or purchasing an individual retirement account.

One-on-One then identifies products offered by the sponsor bank and provides screens on which customers can get more specific information, for instance, they might ask to see certificates of deposit that earned given rates of return over the past 10 years. If consumers cannot get all of their questions answered through the One-on-One interface, they can send an e-mail message to the bank. When they are ready to make purchases, the software provides a means of doing so online.

Intelligent-agent technology promises to offer an even more ambitious means of customizing online shopping. Now in its infancy, agent software allows business Web sites to ask participating customers questions or track their buying preferences and use this information to anticipate future needs. The agent for an online company can then send product announcements or news that consumers might find interesting. Eventually, individual shoppers may maintain their own intelligent agents that would continually scan the Web for information or carry out specific shopping assignments.

One early example of intelligent-agent technology at work can be found on The Firefly Network. New members fill in forms on the screen, rating their preferences for musical groups and movies. Armed with this data, Firefly-a free service-will give them information about music and videos that matches their expressed preferences, and inform them when members with similar interests are available for conversation in the Web site's chat rooms.

9.5 When Pull Comes to Push

In the first heated year or so of Web business, most of the action has revolved around efforts to tap the consumer market. More recently, as the Web proved to be more than a fad, companies have started to buy and sell products and services with one another. Such business-to-business sales make sense because businesspeople typically know what product they're looking for, according to Joseph Bailey, an MIT doctoral student who has written extensively about Internet economics.

Nonetheless, many companies still hesitate to use the Web because of doubts about its reliability. "Businesses need to feel they can trust the pathway between them and the supplier," says senior analyst Blane Erwin of Forrester Research. Some companies are limiting the risk by conducting online transactions only with established business partners who are given access to the company's private intranet.

Another major shift in the model for Internet commerce concerns the technology available for marketing. Until recently, Internet marketing activities have focused on strategies to "pull" customers into sites. In the past year, however, software companies have developed tools that allow companies to "push" information directly out to consumers, transmitting marketing messages directly to targeted customers. Most notably, the Pointcast Network uses a screen saver to deliver a continually updated stream of news and advertisements to subscribers' computer monitors. Subscribers can customize the information they want to receive. By clicking on intriguing advertisements, they proceed directly to a company's Web site. Companies such as Virtual Vineyards are already starting to use similar technologies to push messages to customers about special sales, product offerings, or other events. But push technology has earned the disdain of many Web users. Online culture exalts the notion that the information flowing onto the screen comes there by specific request. Once commercial promotion begins to fill the screen unbidden, the distinction between the Web and television fades. That's a prospect that horrifies Net purists.

But it is hardly inevitable that companies on the Web will need to resort to push strategies to make money. The examples of Virtual Vineyards, Amazon.com, and other pioneers show that a Web site selling the right kind of products with the right mix of interactivity, hospitality, and security will attract online customers. And the cost of computing power continues to free fall, which bodes well for any enterprise setting up shop in silicon. People looking back 5 or 10 years from now may well wonder why so few companies took the online plunge

10

Information Technology in Banking Industry

R.K. Uppal and Rimpi Jatana

The severe crises of 1991 gave birth to the new economic thought in the country. A bundle of measures were taken to remove the various deficiencies and rigidities in the Indian economy. Hence, new economic policy was introduced to mould the Indian economy to the right path. Financial sector reforms and banking sector reforms are the part and parcel of economic reforms, which strengthen the economic reforms. Under the regime of banking sector reforms, IT-Act of 1999 gave new dimensions to the Indian banking industry. IT (ATMs, Smart Cards, Internet-Banking, Tele-Banking, Mobile-Banking, EFTs etc.) has created transformation in banking structure, business process, work culture and human resource development. It has affected the work culture, productivity, profitability and efficiency of the banks to a large extent.

10.1 Introduction

Strengthening the financial sector and improving the functioning of financial markets have been the core objective of the financial sector reforms in India. The significant transformation of the financial system in the country is clearly evident from the changes that have occurred in the financial markets, institutions and products.

The country witnessed in 1990 an economic crisis leading to a fast decline in the GDP, a high rate of inflation, an adverse BOPs due to a widening gap in the current account deficit and a decline in the foreign exchange reserves. The country had to borrow resources from foreign central banks and other foreign government agencies against the pledge of gold so as to avoid a default on international indebtedness. Following were some of the banking sector deficiencies ahead the economy, which were adversely affecting the economic growth of our country.

- productivity and efficiency of the system has suffered;
- its profitability has been eroded;
- several public sector banks and financial institutions have become weak financially;
- some public sector banks have been incurring losses year after year;
- their customer service was poor;
- their work technology was outdated;
- they were unable to meet the challenges of a competitive environment.

Keeping in mind all the above said distortions in the economic, financial and banking sectors, the government of India and the RBI thought it was necessary to introduce reforms in the financial and baking sector also, so as to promote rapid economic growth and development with stability through the process of globalization, liberalization and privatization in the financial system so that the financial system becomes more competitive and gets integrated with the world economy through internationalizations of financial markets in the world.

10.2 Banking Sector Reforms

The government of India, under the chairmanship of Sh. M. Narasimham, an Ex-Governor of RBI, appointed the Narasimham Committee-I (NC-I) in April 1991. The committee examined all the aspects relating to the structural organization, functions and procedures of financial system and submitted its report on November 16, 1991. The NC-I had proposed wide ranging reforms for:

- improving the financial viability of the banks;
- increasing their autonomy from government directions;
- restructuring unviable banks;
- allowing a greater entry of the private sector in banking;

- liberalizing the capital market;
- further improving the operational flexibility & competition among the financial institutions;
- setting up of proper supervisory system.

First Phase of Banking Sector Reforms (1991)

A number of reform initiations have been taken to improve or minimize the distortions impinging upon the efficient and profitable functioning of banks, especially:

1. Reduction in SLR & CRR
2. Transparent guidelines or norms for entry and exit of private sector banks
3. Public sector banks allowed to direct access to capital markets
4. Deregulation of interest rates
5. Branch licensing policy has been liberalized
6. Setting up of Debt Recovery Tribunals
7. Asset classification and provisioning
8. Income recognition
9. Asset Reconstruction Fund (ARF)

These and other measures that have been taken would help the highly regulated and directed banking system to transform itself into one characterized by openness, competition, prudential and supervisory discipline.

Second Phase of Banking Sector Reforms (1998)

The recommendations of the NC-I in 1991 provided the blueprint for the first generation reforms of the financial sector. The period 1992-97 witnessed the laying of foundations for reforms in the banking system.

Cataclysmic changes were taking place in the world economy, coinciding with the movement towards global integration of financial services.

Against such backdrop, the committee NC-II, appointed for the said purpose, generated its report in 1998, and provided the roadmap for the second-generation reform process.

The NC-II with Mr. M. Narasimham as the chairman was constituted on December 26, 1997 to review the banking sector reforms since 1991 and to suggest measures of further strengthening the banking sector .of India. The NC-II examined the second-generation of reforms in terms of three broad interrelated issues:

- action that should be taken to strengthen the foundation of the banking system
- strengthening procedures, upgrading technology and HRD and
- structural changes in the system

These cover the aspects of banking policy, institutional, supervisory and legislative documents. The major recommendations of the committee were:

1. Strengthening banking system
2. Systems and methods of banking
3. Structural issues
4. Integration of financial markets
5. Rural and small scale industrial credit
6. Regulation and supervision

10.3 E-banking

Delivery of bank's services to a customer at his office or home by using electronic technology can be termed as E-banking. The quality, range and price of these e-services decide a bank's competitive position in the industry. The virtual financial services can be largely categorized as follows:

Automated Teller Machines:

- Cash withdrawals
- Details of most recent balance of account
- Mini-statement & Statement ordering facility
- Deposit facility
- Payments to third parties

EFTPoS: EFTPoS card used to initiate transactions:

- Authorization and transaction capture processes take place electronically.
- Transaction confirmed manually.
- Funds not debited electronically.

Remote Banking Services:

- Balance enquiry
- Statement ordering
- Funds transfer (payment) to third parties
- Funds transfer between customer's different accounts
- Order traveler's cheques and other financial instruments.

Services Not Available Through Remote Banking:

- Cash withdrawal
- Cash/ cherub deposit
- Sale of the more complex types of financial services such as life insurance mortgages and (pensions).

Smart Cards:

1. Stored value cards
2. As a replacement for all types of magnetic stripes cards like ATM Cards, Debit/Credit Cards, Charge Cards etc.

- One smart card can contain the functionality of several different types of cards issued by different banks while running different types of networks
- Smart card a truly powerful financial token, giving user access
- Debit facility & Credit facilities
- Electronic purse facilities at national and international level

Internet Banking: The latest wave in IT is Internet banking. It is becoming more obvious that the Internet has unleashed a revolution that is affecting every sphere of life. Internet is an interconnection of computer communication networks spanning the entire globe, crossing all geographical boundaries. Touching lifestyles in every sphere the Net has redefined methods of communication, work, study, education interaction, health, trade and commerce. The Net is changing everything, from the way we conduct commerce, to the way we distribute information. Being an interactive two-way medium, the Net, through innumerable websites, enables participation by individual in B2B and B2C commerce, visits to shopping malls, books-stores, entertainment sides, and so on cyberspace.

10.4 Challenges of E-banking

- **Psychological**
- Conservative
- Hesitation
- Frustration due to lack of technical knowledge

Technological

- Less awareness regarding technology
- Insufficient technology
- Lack of proper infrastructure for the installation of e-delivery channels
- Poor network
- Flaws in design, implementation and monitoring bank's information system

Socio-Economic

- Cost factor
- Vast rural branch network
- Concept of social banking
- Lack of CRM
- Low profitability

Problem of Security in E-banking

- Loss of data due to technical defaults
- Lack of security measures
- Lack of Strong Trust Environment
- Slowness in Adoption of Net by the 40+age Group

10.5 Challenges and Opportunities

Although a lot of reforms have been made in public sector banks, still there is a need to modify the policies of public sector banks. At present they are facing many internal and external challenges, which are hindering their performance, but these banks can convert these challenges into opportunities with care and some modifications. With globalization and changes in the technology, financial markets, world over have become closely integrated. Customers can access their accounts anywhere and banks' customer base is also spread across the world. Deregulation and liberalization has opened up new opportunities for banks but at the same time the pressure of competition have led to narrowing spreads, shrinking margins, consolidation and restructuring.

Increasingly, banks are focusing on core competencies, synchronizing strengths and shedding activities that are not remunerative. The winds of change sweeping across global markets will impact India also, and the Indian financial sector is set to see tremendous transformation in the coming millennium. The face of banking is set to change as banks adopt technology to reduce costs, widen product range for customer convenience and to manage risks. Greater market access to foreign banks, post-WTO will increase competition and as we move towards full capital account convertibility, banks will need to be equipped to handle large and sensitive volatile-capital flows.

Competition: Due to LPG banks are facing a severe competition. To stay ahead in the race, therefore, banks will have to leverage technology for innovative product development including developing sophisticated financial products. While some banks have taken lead in developing new tech-savvy products to beat the competition, also the public sector banks in particular will have to speed up their efforts in this area.

Greater Customer-Orientation: Greater customer-orientation is the only way to retain customer loyalty and stay ahead of competition. In a market-driven strategy of development, consumer preference is paramount. Gone are the days when customers used to come to the doors of the banks and now banks are required to chase the customers. Thus, only banks that are customer-centric and extremely focused on the needs of their clients will succeed and there is need to change the mindset of banks at all levels on this issue.

Public sector banks in particular need to bring about total customer-orientation not only in their products/services but their policies and strategies should also be customer-focused. In fact, they must realize that customer is the only profit center and all others are overheads. Identification of profitable customers, understanding their needs and preferences, improving the delivery systems and reducing the transaction costs for them should become important strategic issues for banks, if they want to survive in the fiercely competitive environment. Enhancing the customer base, cross selling of products/services and strengthening the customer relationship management will be the most important aspect.

Technology: In the deregulated environment, managing a wide range of products on shrinking margins in a fiercely competitive environment and offering top class customer services will create new challenges. In this context, technology will be the key to reduce transaction cost, offering customized products and managing risks. Growing consumer acceptance of e-channels is compelling banks to provide Internet-banking facilities and increasingly, customers are demanding fast, convenient and glitch-free banking services.

However, as banks expand into virtual banking, they will need to pay greater attention to foolproof security arrangements and systems to safeguard against frauds. Supervision and audit of E-banking will have to be strengthened and vigilance against hackers stepped up. Our public sector banks are lagging behind in technology when we compare them with their counterparts. There is a need for vision, strategy, planning and coordination at all levels of the organization.

New Credit Assessment Skills: So far the focus of attention in the Indian banking industry has largely been extending finance to agriculture and manufacturing sectors covering small, medium and large industries. But now banks should capture service class also. Through IT, banks therefore, have to sharpen their credit assessment skills and lay more emphasis in providing finance to the wide range of activities in the services sector.

Management of NPAs: the level of NPAs in the Indian banking industry is a greater concern and thus urgent cleaning up of banks balance that has become a crucial issue. NPAs will have to be reduced drastically and adequate provisioning for bad and doubtful debts will have to be made.

There is a need to have long-term solutions for overcoming this challenge. The internal control systems, risk management systems and systems of catch early warning signals for timely detection of NPAs have to be strengthened by banks. In addition, the role of legal reforms in bringing down the level of NPAs is crucial for speedy settlement of disputes and realization of banks' dues. Also, strengthening the Debt Recovery Tribunals and empowering banks to enforce their change without court intervention will result in expedition recovery of bad debts.

New Basel Capital Accord: The new Basel Accord to modify the existing capital adequacy framework is currently under discussion. Under the revised capital adequacy framework, banks will have to provide for market risk and operational risk besides credit risk. Against the background of government decisions to reduce its shareholding in nationalized banks to 33 pc, maintaining the required level of capital adequacy by the banks could come under strain.

Strong banks will be able to access the capital markets for raising additional equity, but weak banks could face sever problems. But in any case, there will be tremendous pressure on banks to improve their financial performance if they have to attract additional capital.

Profitability will thus have to be improved so that higher dividends are paid to shareholders, capital market perception about public sector banks changes and there is a positive impact on the valuation of shares so that the shares of public sector banks fetch attractive market prices.

WTO and Indian Banking Industry: As WTO provisions came into force, countries including India have to provide greater market access to other countries by eliminating Quantitative Restrictions (QR), regarding tariff barriers and liberalizing the market for financial services. The impact of these developments on various sectors of the Indian economy would be critical.

The banks will have to keep themselves updated on sector specific developments taking place in the world, particularly in countries that are India's major trading partners and advise their corporate clients to help them to prepare for competition with multinational companies.

Corporate Governance: Deregulation and self-regulation go hand-in-hand. RBI has also asked banks to set up specialized committees like Risk Management Committee, Audit Committee, Compensation Committee, Narasimham Committee etc., to ensure the uppermost standards of corporate governance and development of best practices.

A good fiscal management and clear-cut policies affecting various sectors of the economy, can promote corporate governance. The public sector banks, new private sector banks & foreign banks should ensure corporate governance in all the activities and to win the heart of shareholders.

Issue of HRM: Training, development and retaining talented and committed staff is a major emerging challenge before the public sector banks. Today, our employee performance review systems are neither objective nor transparent. They do not differentiate high performers, risk takers and innovators lot from amongst the total staff. Time has come to measure the value of human capital and take urgent steps to ensure it to its optimum level.

Lack of Risk Management: Today, instead of banks managing the risk, risk is managing the banks. A clear understanding of the risk-return profile of each activity of the bank is crucial to ensure the soundness and solvency of the organization. Skill up gradation and preparing a cadre for the risk organization is a major challenge for public sector banks particularly in the wake of high labor turnover.

Lack of Actionable Planning: Lack of planning or ineffective planning is very relevant to public sector banks. Though all the banks have established elaborate performance budgeting system and created MIS, it does not meet the management's present requirements. Basically, the entire planning process is still deposit and credit-oriented, that too, without any cost and yield linkages.

To tackle this challenge an actionable strategic plans which are systematically broken-up into annual plans and performance is strictly reviewed in terms of the targets and accountability is fixed for non-performances.

Non- Accountability: In case of public sector banks, there is non-accountability of profits. No one is responsible. Every bank should fix the responsibility and good performer employees should be honored.

Public Perception: In the ultimate analysis it is the public perception that will decide the future of public sector banks. The perception of customers regarding public sector banks is very poor. Public sector banks should improve their perception by all means to remain competitive in the market.

Customers Expectations: In the era of E-banking and severe competition, the expectations of the bank customers have increased. Due to this banks should offer a broad range of deposits, investment and credit products through diverse distribution channels including upgraded branches, ATMs, telephone and Internet. For this banks should:

- Become more customer centric, offering a wide range of products through multiple delivery channels
- Become proficient in managing assets and liabilities according to risk and return
- Pay greater attention to profitability including cost-reduction and increasing fee-based income.

All these changes require vision, determination and extensive communication across all levels in the organization so that the vision and mission of the banks is communicated and understood down the line and receiver unqualified support.

Mergers and Acquisitions: Today 'size' has become an important issue in financial market world over. Merger on commercial considerations and strategic mergers are the order of the day. One of the possible ways to remain in competition would be mergers and acquisitions. The privately/foreign banks have already set in the trend.

We can say that a constructive and serious measure should be initiated for:

- Better and cheaper access to basic infrastructure requirements such as power, telecommunications i.e. VSAT, leased lines etc.
- Creation of customer's awareness and education for technology adoption are imperative.
- The IT - Act 2000 should be implemented in totality to handle legal issues.
- Converting branches into boutiques catering to the requirements of clients and re-engineering the functions of branch banking using technology and delivery channels.
- Setting up an E-banking group to provide grid principles for risk management of E-banking activities.

10.6 Conclusion

- The paper concludes that transformation is taking place almost in all categories of the banks. This transformation will helpful to cope with new economic and financial policies of the banks.
- IT is playing a crucial role to create the drastic changes in the banking industry particularly in the new private sector and foreign banks.
- The private banks take a big share of cake; our public sector banks are still lagging behind regarding the various financial parameters.
- The immense opportunities are also available for the public sector banks if they change/modify and adopt new policies to combat the different recent challenges.
- It can be concluded that mere introduction of IT alone will not be sufficient to bring necessary performance improvement and to get the competitive edge but intelligent people are required to use such intelligent tools. Thus, even though IT management is a challenge flow in future banking scenario, marketing not technology is going to be the challenge.

10.7 Areas of Future Research

Re-Orienting Structure

1. Issues and solutions in implementing Corporate Governance in banking
2. Reforming capital structure, aspects to be covered are:

- Disinvestments of PSBs
- Raising capital from the market
- Foreign direct investment (FDI)

3. An appropriate banking model for India:

- Universal banking Vs. Narrow banking
- Adopting international best practices i.e. Basel – II

Re-Engineering Operations

- Marketing of financial services: Product, Process and Pricing
- Retail Banking
- Risk Management including regulatory and environmental risks
- Legal challenges

Harnessing Facilitators

1. Technology

- Issues in identification and cost-benefit analysis of appropriate technology – Case Studies
- Disaster Recovery Management

2. Human Resource Development

- Preparing for the cultural transformation
- Knowledge management

Bibliography

Arora, Kalpana (2003), 'Indian Banking: Managing Transformation through IT', IBA Bulletin, Vol. XXV, No. 3, (March), pp. 134-138.

Avasthi, G.P.M. (2000-01), 'Information Technology in Banking: Challenges for Regulators', Prajnan, Vol. XXIX, No. 4, pp. 3 -17

Bajaj, K.K. (2000), 'E-Commerce Issues in the Emerging Hi -Tech. Banking Environment', The Journal of The Indian Institute of Bankers, (Jan- March).

Bakshi, S. (2003), 'Corporate Governance in Transformation Times', IBA Bulletin,

Bhasin, T.M. (2001), 'E-Commerce in Indian Banking', IBA Bulletin, Vol. XXIII, Nos. 4 & 5, (April – May).

E- Banking', IBA Bulletin, (January).

Ganesh, S. (2001), 'Frauds in A Computerized Environment', IBA Bulletin, Vol. XXIII,

Garg, I.K. (2003), 'Indian Banking in Transition: Some Management Challenges', IBA Bulletin, Vol. XXV, No. 3, (March), pp. 121-123

Gupta, R P. (2001), 'Banking in the New Millennium: Strategic Management Issues', IBA Bulletin, Vol. XXIII, No. 3 (March), pp.38-45

Jalan, B. (2003), 'Strengthening Indian Banking and Finance: Progress and Prospectus', IBA Bulletin, Vol. XXV, No. 3, (March).

Kulkarni, R. V. (2000), 'Changing Face of Banking from Brick and Mortar Banking to

Mohan, R. (2003), 'Transforming Indian Banking: In Search of a Better Tomorrow', IBA Bulletin, Vol. XXV, No. 3, (March).

Nair, S.N. (2000), 'E-Commerce and The Emergence of E-banking', IBA Bulletin, Vol. XXII, No. 10, (October), No. 12, (December), pp. 19-25

Sandhu, H.S. & Soch (2003) 'Impact of Information Technology on the Indian Banking Sector', Edited Book, Economic Reforms in India – From First to Second Generation and Beyond, Deep & Deep Publications, New Delhi, pp. 413 - 422

Shapiro, C (2000), 'Will E-Comm. Erode Liberty', Harvard Business Review, (May- June).

Shastri, R.V (2001), 'Technology for Banks in India- Challenges', IBA Bulletin, Vol. XXIII, No. 3, (March), pp. 23-45

Trivedi, A. K. (2003), 'Indian Banking: Managing Transformation', IBA Bulletin, Vol. XXV, No. 3, (March) Vol. XXV, No. 3, (March).

11

E-banking in India: Dream vs. Reality

Shiwani Gupta and Neetu Khanna

Electronic Banking is not out to change your money habits. It simply uses today's technology to give you the option of bypassing the time-consuming, paper-based aspects of traditional banking in order to manage your finances more quickly and efficiently.

11.1 Introduction

Finance function is the backbone of business transactions. Business transactions are undergoing day-by-day technological change. So, traditional form of Finance Function is not enough to cope-up with pace of changing technological scenario. The comprehensive form of this technological change in finance function is E-banking. E-banking is of recent origin, especially in India, it is still in its adolescent age.

Generally speaking, E-banking means providing banking products and services through electronic signals.

"E-banking means offering, supplying & delivering banking products and services through various electronic delivery channels via electronic devices"

11.2 Banking Products and Services under E-banking

Basic Services

- Account enquiry
- Funds transfer
- Bill presentment and payment
- **Value-added Services**
- Cash management
- Credit and debit cards

- Customer correspondence
- Foreign exchange transactions
- Demat holdings
- Online trading
- Account opening
- Requests and intimation
- Financial advice
- Insurance
- Tax services
- Shopping
- Standing instructions like stop payment of some cheque, tax payment electricity bill payment, insurance premium payment, collecting receipts from customers' business clients etc.
- Investments
- Asset management services 16.brokerage.

11.3 E-banking Devices

Telephone: The customers interact with the bank for various services over phone. There will be no charge for dialing to the toll free number provide by the bank Tele-banking, also known 'Voice over Phone', is considered under anywhere banking. The bank installs a voice response system. The customer identifies himself to the system by entering (dialing) his PIN number. This ensures confidentiality of the affairs of the customers, apart from proper authentication. The customer dials the free toll telephone number and is guided by a voice response for each banking service namely:

- Balance in the account
- Transaction status, e.g. whether cheque deposited is cleared or not.
- Request for issue of cheque book is registered.
- Request for issue of bank statement is registered.

In normal course all above activities would have involved customers visit to a branch and this anywhere banking a tele-banking has improved banking services and enabled remote banking.

Mobile: Mobile Banking can be divided into two broad categories of facilities:

- **Alert Facility:** Mobile Banking Alerts facility keeps you informed about the significant transactions in your Accounts. It keeps you updated wherever you go.
- **Request Facility:** Mobile Banking Requests facility enables you to query for your account balance.

Personal Computer: PC Banking allows the customers to access the information regarding their bank accounts through a dial up connections. They can also download the information and process it in their own manners. It is different from Internet banking in the sense that Internet banking is done over a highly accessible public networks, whereas PC banking is accessible just to banks' customers.

ATM: Automated Teller machines facilitate 24 X 7 X 365 hour's banking, i.e. Any-time banking it allows its customers to withdraw or deposit funds, check account balances, transfer funds and check statement information.

Kiosks in action	
Banking	Account information, printing DDs
Internet	For Internet access
Movies	For issuing tickets
Digital mini-lab	For printing photographs
Vending	For buying DVDs, music, ringtones, games
Security	For scanning visitor cards; in-built security camera function

Kiosk Machine: Initially their use was restricted to distributing information, but now they are becoming more interactive, Computer kiosks can store data locally, or they can retrieve data from a remote server over a network. Kiosks can be used to provide information, which facilitate e-governance, or for facilitating online transactions, or collecting cash in exchange for commodities (your basic vending machine)

POS (Point of Sale) is a device by which sales transactions can be directly debited to the customer's bank account at the point of sale, through the use of a debit card (sometimes the same card used with Automatic Teller Machines). The customer's card is swiped through a card reader or inserted into chip reader and the merchant usually enters the amount of the transaction before the customer enters their account and PIN. There is usually a short delay while the POS terminal contacts the server (over a phone line or mobile connection) before a message of Accepted or Declined is returned. Often, at peak shopping times (for example the last shopping day before Christmas), the system can become overloaded and the delay will become extended or even time out.

11.4 Delivery Channels

Internet: The Internet banking is changing the banking industry and is having the major effects on banking relationships. It is an improvement over PC banking. The Internet provides the banks with the ability to deliver the products and services to the customer. Who has access to public networks at the cost, which is less than any other existing method of delivery? Customer can avail this service by just logging into banks' websites with a click of mouse.

ATM Card: To make the use of ATM, customer needs a special ATM card and he is allotted a PIN (Personal Identification Number), which is not shown on face of the card. The card must be inserted into the machine and PIN is typed in. The machine will validate the code no. And if correct will allow the access to the bank's computer boot to check the account balance, to withdraw the cash, to deposit the money and other facilities.

CARDs: Credit cards represent a step in the direction of an electronic fund transfer system. It is a card, which provides right to its holder to use it from making the payment against purchases. Customer needs not to make immediate cash payment.

Debit card is just similar to credit card with basic difference that debit card holder must has credit balance in his bank account.

11.5 Present Status of Implementation of E-banking Services

Different banks are in different stages of implementation of E-banking. All the banks can be divided into three stages:

Information websites: these websites provide information on financial services offered in bank branches and most of banks in India provide such websites.

Electronic and Internet banking: customers can do basic banking transactions like opening an account, payment of utility bills, checking their balance and transactions.

E-commerce and E-banking: Banks become electronic market place where customers can buy and sell through banks' payment gateway.

The basis advantage of E-banking over traditional banking is cost saving.

A cost comparison study done by IBM global services consulting group clearly shows the advantage of using Internet as medium for banking services over other traditional mediums. As per the recent survey, traditional banks spend 60 per cent of the revenue generated to run a branch whereas the cost of providing same services via Internet comes out to be only 15 per cent. This is a huge savings for banks and consumer. Definitely the consumer is the principal beneficiary of the Internet Banking. He will be access the same services with more efficiency at low cost. E banking will have two-fold effect, first, it will reach the remote consumer and second it will create the awareness among consumer about benefits of investment in different financial products. Investment in-turns boost the financial markets and economy. A research shows that a large urban population use Internet for gathering information about different financial products like personal loan, credit card, insurance etc., thus reducing cost of printing, promotion and distribution for citizen it's transparent & efficient.

11.6 Review of Literature

Singh and Malhotra (2004) found that there has constantly been a literature gap on the issue in India. The purpose of this paper is to help fill significant gaps in knowledge about the Internet banking landscape in India. The paper presents data, drawn from a survey of commercial banks websites, on the number of commercial banks that offer Internet banking and on the products and services they offer. It investigates the profile of commercial banks that offer Internet banking, using univariate statistical analysis, relative to other commercial banks with respect to profitability, cost efficiency, and other 1characteristics. By the end of first quarter, 2004, differences between Internet and non-Internet banks had begun to emerge in funding, in sources of income and expenditures and in measures of performance. It was also found that the profitability and offering of Internet banking does not have any significant correlation.

Chang (2003) has examined behaviour of firms (banks) and consumers (banks' customers) in the event of a new technology (internet banking) introduction. The determinants of consumer adoption of Internet banking are characterized using survey data from Korea in both static and dynamic framework. I find evidence that adoption of Internet banking is influenced by sex, age, marital status, degree of exposure to Internet banking, and the characteristics of the banks. A duration analysis shows no evidence of first mover advantage (order effects) in Internet banking whilst the largest bank (rank effects) in commercial banking remains dominant in Internet banking. The results imply that social norm effects dominate the Internet banking adoption.

Aggarwal (2002) There are five key areas in banking where technology has contributed the most are: Product Development, Market Infrastructure, Risk Control and Market Research [Online banks can be classified as Fully Traditional banks, Traditional banks with Internet presence and fully Virtual banks The success of Traditional banks with Internet presence is eminent not only in India but also anywhere in the world. India has an extensive banking network, consisting of rural and urban banks. Largely speaking the most of the Indian banks are still public sector banks. New age private sector banks like ICICI, HDFC, UTI are fast becoming choice of citizens in urban areas where technology penetration is high.

Corrocher (2002) investigated the determinants of the adoption of Internet technology for the provision of banking services in the Italian context and also studied the relationship between the Internet banking and the traditional banking activity, in order to understand if these two systems of financial services delivery are perceived as substitutes or complements by the banks. From the results of the empirical analysis, banks seem to perceive Internet banking as a substitute for the existing branching structure, although there is also some evidence that banks providing innovative financial services are more inclined to adopt the innovation than traditional banks

Furst et. al. (2002) provided a comparative study of Internet and non-Internet banks in U.S. and found that institutions with Internet banking outperformed non-Internet banks in profitability. Also, banks in all categories of size offering Internet banking tended to rely less on interest yielding activities and deposits than non-Internet banks do.

Hasan (2002) found that online home banking has emerged as a significant strategy for banks to attract customers. Almost 75 percent of the Italian banks have adopted some form of Internet banking during the period 1993-2000. It also found that the higher likelihood of adopting active Internet banking activities is by larger banks, banks with higher involvement in off-balance sheet activities, past performance and higher branching network

Jalan (2002) Information and Communication Technologies (ICT's) has bought the fundamental revolution in banking sector.

Janice et. al. (2002) based on interviews with four banks in Hong Kong noted that banks view the Internet as being a supplementary distribution channel for their products and services in addition to other forms of distribution channels such as Automated Teller Machines (ATMs), phones, mobile phones and bank branches. Basic transactions and securities trading are the most popular types of operations that customers carry out in Internet banking.

Jasimuddin (2001) found that within one year of the introduction of Internet service in Saudi Arabia, Saudi banks had at least decided on their Internet presence. 73 per cent of the Saudi banks possessed their own web sites and 25 per cent of the web sites were offering full services over Internet. The banks viewed the Internet as a key alternative delivery channel

MIT (2001) Five years from now, majority of the transactional services will be provided by way of Internet. Net-based banking comes at only 10 per cent of the operating costs of conventional banking practices and services. As banks are going to play a key role in IT enabled public services involving electronic money transactions we feel that cooperative banks should consider NET-Banking in a big way.

Suganthi et. al. (2001) conducted the review of Malaysian banking sites and revealed that all domestic banks were having a web presence. Only 4 of the ten major banks were with transactional sites. The remaining sites were at informational level. There are various psychological and behavioral issues as trust, security of Internet transactions, reluctance to change and preference for human interface which appear to impede the growth of Internet banking

Aggarwal N, Aggarwal R, Sharma (2000) explore the implementation techniques of Activity-Based Costing (ABC) in the banking sector on the example of an Estonian bank in order to analyze the cost structure for traditional and electronic channel transactions. The article shows how it is possible to implement ABC in banking and proves empirically those electronic channels help reduce the costs of both banks and their clients

Guru et. al. (2000) examined the various electronic channels utilized by the local Malaysian banks and also accessed the consumers reactions to these delivery channels. It was found that

Internet banking was nearly absent in Malaysian banks due to lack of adequate legal framework and security concerns. However over 60 percent of the respondents were having Internet access at home and thus represented a positive indication for PC based and Internet banking in future.

Sullivan (2000) found that Internet banks in 10th Federal Reserve District incurred higher expenses but also generated higher fee income and concluded that the measures of profitability for Internet banks are similar to those of the non-Internet banks.

Diniz (1998) reported a survey of web sites of banks in USA. It was found that most of the bank websites were basic and intermediate level. No website was found to be of advanced level.

Egland (1998) conducted the first important study that estimated the number of U.S. banks offering Internet banking and analyzed the structure and performance characteristics of these banks. They have found no evidence of major differences in the performance of the group of banks offering Internet banking activities compared to those that do not offer such services.

Furst et. al. (1998) a U.S. based study found out a significant shift by consumers and businesses to electronic payments. In response to developments in electronic payments and remote banking, banks have greatly increased their investment in technology, particularly in retail banking. The gains from technological advancements in banking and payments are likely to be substantial, both from the point of view of individual financial institutions and economy-wide. In this environment, banks should review and, if necessary, adjust their risk management practices in tandem with upgrading their technology activities.

Booz Allen Hamilton (1997) conducted a global survey covering 386 retail and corporate banking institutions in 42 countries to assess the strategic impact of Internet banking on the financial service industry. According to the study, there is a huge perception gap between North American/European banks and Japanese banks regarding the future of Internet banking.. The study also indicates the rapid growth potential of Internet banking.

Many of the banks that responded have plans to upgrade the functionality of their Internet service offerings.

11.7 Analysis of Results

On the basis of survey conducted, the following analysis has been made:

Banking Habits

These have been analyzed on the basis of fact that whether respondents have bank accounts or not

Response	**per cent**
Yes	97
No	3

The survey shows that most of the respondents have bank accounts (97 per cent)

Preference of Bank

Bank preference has been judged by seeing the fact that whether their bank is public, private or any other bank

Response	**per cent**
Public bank	84
Private bank	32
Other	6

Survey shows that 84 per cent of respondents have preferred public sector banks. This further has been analyzed in the direction of multiplicity of bank accounts. Results show that 64 per cent of respondents have only one account, i.e. they do not have habit of having account in more than one bank.

Awareness of E-banking

Response	**per cent**
Very Well	48
Somewhat	45
Not at all	7

Result shows that 93.5 per cent of respondents have knowledge of the concept either very well (48 per cent) or somewhat (45 per cent).

Technical Knowledge of the Concept:

Response	per cent
Yes	94
No	6

Result shows that 81 per cent of the respondents technically know the concept and they know E-banking includes ATM, I-banking, EFT, EDI, Tele-banking and Mobile banking.

Knowledge of Banks Facilities

Response	per cent
ATM	45
I-Banking	32
EFT	19
Mobile	32
All	32

Data shows that 45 per cent of the respondents have knowledge of ATM facilities as E-banking service provided by their bank followed by I-banking (32 per cent). However, the true picture is far away from their knowledge.

Services Actually Availed By Respondents

Response	per cent
ATM	81
I-Banking	39
EFT	29
Mobile	19
Nil	23

Analysis shows that 81 per cent of the respondents use ATM facility followed by 39 per cent availing I-BANKING.

Satisfaction of Respondents

Response	per cent
Very Much	10
Satisfied	61
Somewhat	26
Not at all	nil
Can't say	3

Result shows that most of the respondents (97 per cent) are satisfied with the quality of services provide by their particulars banks. However, 26 per cent of the respondents are not fully satisfied. The respondents, who are not satisfied or less satisfied grumble regarding unreliability of software, non-regular working of ATM, delay made by banks and extra processing charges imposed by banks.

	ATM	EFT	EDI	Online Banking	Tele-Banking
Allahabad Bank	Y	Y	Y	Y	
Andhra Bank	Y	Y	Y	Y	Y
BoB	Y			Y	Y
BoI	Y	Y		Y	Y
Centurian Bank of Pb	Y	Y	Y	Y	Y
Bahrat Overseas	Y	Y	Y	Y	Y
Canara Bank	Y	Y	Y	Y	Y
Dena Bank	Y	Y	Y	Y	Y
HDFC	Y	Y	Y	Y	Y
ICICI	Y	Y	Y	Y	Y
IDBI	Y	Y		Y	Y
Indian Bank	Y	Y	Y	Y	Y
Indian Overseas Bank	Y	Y	Y	Y	
OBC	Y	Y	Y	Y	
SBI	Y	Y	Y	Y	
PNB	Y	Y		Y	
Syndicate Bank	Y	Y	Y	Y	
UCO	Y	Y	Y	Y	
UBI	Y		Y	Y	
ABN AMRO	Y	Y	Y	Y	Y
Bank of Rajasthan	Y		Y		
HSBC	Y	Y	Y		Y
ING vyasa	Y	Y	Y	Y	Y
Standard Chartered	Y	Y	Y	Y	Y
City Bank	Y	Y	Y	Y	Y

(Source: Websites of various banks. 'y' implies bank provides the service)

Inter Bank Services Comparison by Respondents

Response	per cent
Yes	26
No	74

Analyses reveal that 74 per cent of respondents are not interested in comparing services of their banks.

The respondents who compared the services report that private sector bank are better than public sector banks in terms of processing time, efficiency and quickness.

Responsibility for Dissatisfaction

Response	per cent
Fault in System	3
Fault in bank	26
Can't Say	71

Most of the Respondents (71 per cent) are unable to hold responsible either a particular bank or system itself for their dissatisfaction however 8 per cent respondents: consider fault in services of their particular bank for dissatisfaction. The reason for the same may be that they have one bank account only and they do not compare their own bank with other bank.

11.8 Findings

The main findings of the survey are:

1. In India 'Brick cum Click' form of E-banking is existing, i.e. there is no virtual bank (wholly electronic, having no physical building).-
2. People have banking habit. And they preferred public sector banks
3. People do not have habit of having account in more than one bank.
4. Respondents are found to have knowledge of the concept they know e banking includes ATM, I-banking, EFT, EDI, Tele-banking and Mobile banking.
5. People are not fully aware of the services provided by their own bank except ATM facilities

6. ATM facility's found to be most popular E-banking service availed by the customers followed by availing I-BANKING.
7. Respondents are satisfied with the quality of services provide by their particulars banks Respondents are not interested in comparing services of their banks.
8. Respondents who are not satisfied or less satisfied with E-banking services provided by their bank, grumble regarding unreliability of software, non-regular working of ATM, delay made by banks and extra processing charges imposed by banks. The respondents: who compared the services report that private sector bank are better than public sector banks in terms of processing time, efficiency and quickness.
9. People are unaware of the actual accuse. They are unable to hold responsible either a particular bank or system itself for their dissatisfaction. However few respondents: consider fault in services of their particular bank to be responsible for dissatisfaction. The reason for the same may be that they have one bank account only and they do not compare their own bank with other bank

11.9 Recommendations

1. Awareness must be created among the bank client of the concept.
2. People should shift from Brick banking to Click Banking.
3. Banks should improve their services in term of processing time.
4. Banks should have proper technical staff to handle E-banking system.
5. Banks should provide ATM at more places.
6. E-banking services should be provided either free of cost or at the cost less than the amount that would otherwise be involved in the banking transaction.
7. In order to enhance transparency, alerts should be provided to customers of each banking transaction (through mail, SMS or post) free of cost at the initiative of bank itself.

11.10 Conclusion

From above discussion it is clear that e- banking has worked as change agent. It has changed the facet of traditional banking. The primary drivers of electronic banking includes, in order of primacy are:

- Improve customer access.
- Facilitate the offering of more services.
- Increase customer loyalty.
- Attract new customers.
- Provide services offered by competitors.
- Reduce customer attrition.

Further analysis shows the rosy picture that people have knowledge of the concept and they are availing it also. However facts are only confined to particular sample and furthermore sample has been drawn on the basis of judgment technique of sampling (i.e. questionnaires have been got filled from the persons who are seemed to have knowledge of the concept.) This was due to reason that people are not aware of the concept and they are unable to give the desired information. So, technology in banking sector is yet to overlap traditional system.

References

Agarwal N, Agarwal R, Sharma P "Ebanking for Comprehensive E-democracy: An Indian Discernment" www.JIBC.com/e-banking, 2000

Bimil Jalan, "Strengthening Indian Banking and Finance - Progress and Prospects", The Bank Economist Conference, India, 2002.

Booz-Allen & Hamilton, Inc. (1997)."Booz-Allen's Worldwide Survey Revealed A Huge Perception Gap Between Japanese and American/European Banks Regarding Internet Banking."

Chang.y, "Dynamics of Banking Technology Adoption: An Application to Internet Banking" Department of Economics, University of Warwick, January 2003

Corrocher, N. (2002), "Does Internet banking substitute traditional banking? Empirical Evidence from Italy," Working Paper, CESPRI, No. 134, November.

Diniz, E (1998). "Web Banking In USA," Journal of Internet Banking and Commerce, Vol.3, No. 2, June.

Egland, Kori L., Karen Furst, Daniel E. Nolle, Douglas Robertson (1998). "E-banking over the Internet", Quarterly Journal, Vol. 17, No. 4, Office of Comptroller of the Currency, December.

Furst, K; Lang, W., William and Nolle, E., Daniel (2002). "Internet Banking: Developments and Prospects," Working Paper, Center for Information Policy Research, Harvard University, April.

Hasan, I., (2002). "Do Internet Activities Add Value? The Italian Bank Experience", Working Paper, Federal Reserve Bank of Atlanta, New York University.

Janice, David and Dennis (2002), "Click and Mortar of Retail Banking A Case Study in Hong Kong," Nanyang Business School, Nanyang Technological University.

Official web site of Ministry of Information Technology, Government of India. http://www.mit.gov.in/eg/home.asp, 2003

Singh.b;Malhotra .p "Adoption of Internet Banking: An Empirical Investigation of Indian Banking Sector"www.JIBC.com/e-banking,2004.

12

Internet Banking: Boon or Bane

Nitu Gupta

There is little doubt that the Internet has revolutionized the entire communication system. As much as banking involves communication in one way or the other, banks have joined the communication bandwagon. As in any new venture there are setbacks in terms of issue of security and associated costs. As a consequence banks are working towards remedying these shortcomings so as to take full advantage of the digital revolution.

12.1 Introduction

Vinton Cerf, the father of the Internet, envisioned an online environment populated by billions. The Internet, which was born in 1969, would certainly 'catch fire', according to Cerf. Cerf estimated that three billion users would be online by 2010, and the number of devices online could be anywhere from six billion to 30 billion by 2020 responding. The Internet reached 50 million consumers within 4 years while the radio took nearly 28 years.

Banking is an industry that is based on intensive information, and transactions in banking can normally be consummated without any physical exchange. These ingredients have made banking a perfect passenger for the Internet vehicle. However, in the initial stages Internet banking had to go through hard times and failures. As a result, customers do not seem to be much excited about Internet banking. In fact, an article in the *Euromoney* magazine quoted Internet banking as "Click, click – you are dead" (Irvine, 1999)

12.2 Types of Internet Banking

Currently, there are three basic kinds of Internet banking that are being employed in the marketplace:

Information: This is the most basic level of Internet banking. The bank has marketing information about its products and services on a stand-alone server. This level of Internet banking service can be provided by the bank itself or by sourcing it out. Since the server or Web site may be vulnerable to alteration, appropriate controls must therefore be in place to prevent unauthorized alterations to data in the server or web site.

Communication: This type of Internet banking allows interaction between the bank's systems and the customer. It may be limited to electronic mail, account inquiry, loan applications, or static file updates. The risk is higher with this configuration than with the earlier system and therefore appropriate controls need to be in place to prevent, monitor, and alert management of any unauthorized attempt to access bank's internal network and computer systems. Under this system the client makes a request to which the bank subsequently responds. It works on the same principle as the e-mail.

Transaction: Under this system of Internet banking customers are allowed to execute transactions. Relative to the information and communication types of Internet banking, this system possesses the highest level of risk architecture and must have the strongest controls. Customer transactions can include accessing accounts, paying bills, transferring funds, etc. These possibilities demand very stringent security.

12.3 Growth in Internet Banking

Transaction Multiplier Effect: The myriad possibilities of settling bills, transferring funds (inter/intra bank etc) and trading in securities; all done online, has further encouraged customers to patronize the online system. The increasing numbers of patrons and the consequent rise in revenues have further spurred financial institutions to establish ever expanding infrastructures to support more online activities.

Faster Launch Cycles: The development of Internet banking encourages financial institutions to frequently launch new programs in response to customer preferences and technology innovations. Among the popular enhancements to Internet banking services include improved navigation, integrating multiple services into single systems, viewing of returned checks, onsite purchase of retail goods, seamless integration with e-commerce retail sites, and use of Extensible Markup Language (XML). Such potential tends to further encourage participation.

Poaching of High Net-worth Customers and Competition: Online brokerage firms are beginning to poach high net-worth customers from online banks. Such customers are a segment of the banking population, which includes more than six million U.S. households with a net worth of more than US$ 1 billion. This segment is growing at a rate of 13 percent annually (Internet Banking Solution, 2001). This kind of intense competition further pushes financial institutions to improve their systems which results in attracting more customers.

Geographical Reach: A brick and mortar bank is limited by its geographical reach but the same cannot be said of Internet banks. Internet banking by its very nature is borderless. This new delivery channel can now reach out to areas and regions which have hitherto remained unexplored.

Branding Possibilities: Internet banking technology and products can provide a means for banks to develop and maintain an ongoing relationship with their customers by offering easy access to a broad array of products and services. The results of these efforts are enhanced by capitalizing on brand identification and providing a broad range of financial services, which tends to build customer loyalty, cross-sell, and enhance repeat business.

12.4 Advantages of Internet Banking

The benefits of Internet banking are plentiful as witnessed by the consequential reaction of a tremendous rise in usage and application. The potential appears to be unlimited ranging from virtual banks to e-cash.

Perfect Information: Internet makes perfect information available to all market participants by bringing about efficiencies in the search process. For buyers of banking services, there are sites that aggregate information on product offerings from different providers at a single location. By merely making information available to customers about multiple providers, the Internet performs the function of dismantling the oligopoly of a few providers and bringing about a structure favorable towards perfect competition. A good example of this would be e-loan. It allows potential borrowers to search and compare the offerings of thousands of providers. On the other hand, seeking out bank branches, researching product catalogues and making phone calls cannot achieve this function with the same level of efficiency. Eliminating the agent's commission effects a further reduction in mortgage costs. E-loans also allow for the monitoring of mortgages over its lifetime and alert the borrower to cheaper refinance options whenever available. Perfect information would be available to the bank as well. The Internet makes it less likely, for example, for an individual to hide a bad credit history from prospective providers and to beat the system by switching providers frequently. This entire means that there is limited room for hearsay, verbal/oral accounts, and its related subjectivity. In short the Internet has resulted in a wider dissemination of quality information.

Perfect Competition: Successful dot. com companies such as eBay for instance, offer visitors the ability to directly participate in all transactions such as online auctions. More than 60 million auctions have been completed on eBay since its inception in 1995 and in January 2000, the number of daily visitors to eBay on an average basis set a new record of 1.782 million (Singhal, 2003).

eBay's success is mainly due to its offering to visitors an electronic market place that is tending towards perfect competition. This is achieved by two means. The first is through the aggregation of buyers and sellers and also through the provision of a search function platform. The second is by bringing about efficiency in determining price that is enabled by the online auction mechanism which makes pricing transparent and also makes it dynamic since it is driven by near perfect market conditions of demand and supply.

Similarly, by creating competition among the providers of capital, the Internet helps companies raise money at much finer spreads. Also banks using the Internet have pioneered the use of online auction to price Initial Public Offerings (IPOs). In this manner market forces are given greater prominence thus ensuring conditions for perfect or near perfect competition.

12.5 Disadvantages of Internet Banking

There are always two sides to a coin. Similarly Internet banking too has a 'bane' side to it. The bane lies in its inexorable slide towards higher risk from various facets of bank operations. Risk is the potential that unexpected events may have an adverse impact on the banks earnings. Internet banking risks consists of risk associated with credit, interest rate, transaction, etc. These risks are not mutually exclusive but invariably all of these are associated with Internet banking

Credit Risk: Credit risk is the risk to earning and eventually capital, arising from a borrower's failure to meet the terms of a credit contract with the bank or otherwise to perform as agreed. It is found in all activities where success depends on counterparty, issuer, or borrower performance. It arises any time bank findings are extended, committed, invested, or otherwise exposed through actual or implied contractual agreements, whether on or off the bank's balance sheet.

Internet banking provides the opportunity for banks to expand their geographic range. Customers can reach a given institution from literally anywhere in the world. In dealing with customers over the Internet, absent of any personal contact, it is challenging for institutions to verify the bona fide of their customers, which is an important element in making sound credit decisions. Verifying collateral and perfecting security agreements can also be challenging with out-of-area borrowers.

Unless properly managed, Internet banking could lead to a concentration in out-of-area credits. Moreover, the question of which state's or country's laws control an Internet relationship is still very much at an infancy stage of development.

Effective management of a portfolio of loans obtained through the Internet requires that effective policies, processes, and practices are in place to control the risk associated with such loans.

Interest Rate Risk: Interest rate risk is the risk to earnings arising from movements in interest rates. From an economic perspective, a bank focuses on the sensitivity of the value of its assets, liabilities and revenues to changes in interest rates. Interest rate risk arises from differences between the timing of rate changes and the timing of cash flows (repricing risk); from changing rate relationships among different yield curves affecting bank activities (basis risk); from changing rate relationships across the spectrum of maturities (yield curve risk); and from interest-related options embedded in bank products (options risk) (Comptroller's Handbook, 1999). Evaluation of interest rate risk must consider the impact of complex illiquid hedging strategies or products, and also the potential impact that changes in interest rates will have on fee income. In situations where trading is managed separately, it refers to structural positions and not trading portfolios. The attracting of inflow (deposits) done instantaneously and independently from outflow (loans) with rates moving in between could cause major upheavals if not managed properly. Of course this risk existed even prior to the Internet era but real time implications due to Internet applications have exacerbated the risk.

Liquidity Risk: Liquidity risk is the uncertainty arising from a bank's inability to meet its obligations when they are due, without incurring unacceptable losses. Liquidity risk includes the inability to manage unplanned changes in market conditions affecting the ability of the bank to liquidate assets quickly and with minimal loss in value.

Internet banking increases deposit volatility from customers who maintain accounts solely on the basis of rates or terms. Increased monitoring of liquidity and changes in deposits and loans may be warranted depending on the volume and nature of Internet account activities. In a nutshell, the Internet allows all transactions to occur in real time. The management must therefore be prepared for immediate changes and consequently immediate solutions.

Transaction Risk: Transaction risk is the current and prospective risk to earnings and capital arising from fraud, error, the inability to deliver products or services, the failure to maintain a competitive position and services, and the inability to manage information properly. This risk is evident in each product and service offered and encompasses product development and delivery, transaction processing, systems development, computing systems, complexity of products and services, and the internal control environment (Comptroller's Handbook, 1999). A high level of transaction risk may exist with Internet banking products, particularly if those lines of business are not adequately planned, implemented, and monitored. Banks that offer financial products and services through the Internet must be able to meet their customer's expectations. Banks must also ensure they have the right product mix and capacity to deliver accurate, timely, and reliable services to develop a high level of confidence in their brand name. Customers who conduct business over the Internet are likely to have little tolerance for errors or omissions from financial institutions that do not have sophisticated internal controls to manage their Internet banking business. Likewise, customers will expect continuous availability of the product and Web pages that are easy to navigate.

Software to support various Internet banking functions is provided to the customer from a variety of sources. Banks may support customers using customer-acquired or bank-supplied browsers or Personal Financial Manager (PFM) software. Good communications between banks and their customers will help manage expectations on the compatibility of various PFM software products Internet banking products connected to a robust network may actually make this easier because back up capabilities can be spread over a wide geographic location. Security issues should be considered when the institution develops its contingency and business resumption plans. In such situations however, security and internal controls at the back-up location should be as sophisticated as those at the primary processing site. High levels of security and control systems will be a key expectation of customers and this will most likely differentiate success levels among financial institutions selling Internet products and services (Comptroller's Handbook, 1999).

12.6 Opportunities for Internet Banking

Internet banking as an alternative delivery channel offers many opportunities for growth and development of the financial institutions. Financial institutions have begun to realize that although the Internet is simply a delivery channel it is nevertheless an extremely powerful one. Therefore, financial institutions are investing in electronic Customer Relationship Management (eCRM) solutions that span across all channels, with the goal of strengthening customer loyalty and increasing fee-based transactions. In order to achieve this, eCRM solutions track customer interactions across channels, analyzing the aggregate data that will reveal patterns about customer usage of financial products. Consequently, by using this information, financial institutions can generate business rules that define as to which type of offers need to be made to customers at various times of their lives. Increasingly, financial institutions make offers through all channels, tracking the results to make business strategies even more effective.

Online Mortgage Applications: Until recently, online applications were restricted to credit cards and small loans. Now more people are beginning to apply for mortgages online. However, the volume is growing slowly due to inadequate online customer support. Experts forecast the number of home purchasers researching mortgages online to reach 25 to 30 percent. While many may review this availability the actual closing of deals may only reach 6 percent per annum (Internet Banking Solutions, 2001).

Electronic Cheques for B2B Payments: Electronic cheques have become more popular for retail purchases but until now have had little impact on business payments. It is expected that businesses such as retailers would turn cheques into ACH transactions to retain compatibility with their accounts payable systems (Internet Banking Solutions, 2001

Total Reliability Risk: As with most other Internet ventures, an exclusive reliance on virtual channels is probably not a very wise move. A strategy of combining brick and mortar with click and avatar is probably more viable. There are transactions such as balance enquiry that are ideally suited for the Internet. But transactions such as working capital loan applications are more detailed and personal discussions may be necessary. In the latter, the absence of a physical channel is a problem. Figure 5 shows various banking transaction that are suitable for Internet banking and the expected level of physical contact. Transactions such as bill payment can be efficiently conducted entirely online. Credits to accounts such as those for salary can also be online through electronic credits.

However, even if it is considered that Internet banking works well for certain types of credits, account holders also receive cheques that need to be deposited physically. The process followed by online banks as regards to cheque deposits is to install cheque accepting machines (ATM prototype) which collect cheques, clear them and credit the proceeds into the depositors' accounts. Unfortunately, cheques do not seem to be going away in any hurry as Americans alone write approximately 69 billion cheques a year (Singhal, 2003)

There are also deep psychological links between money and financial services that create inertia in terms of adopting new technologies. For example the U.S. Federal Reserve Board predicts that the number of cheques written in the United States will actually rise and not fall (Singhal, 2003). This is the expectation despite all the improvements and developments in Internet banking. It looks as though convincing people that holding and transacting money in electronic form is equally secure as using paper is going to be a never ending process.

Online Credit Card Payments: Credit cards will remain the dominant consumer Internet payment for the future. While online debit and electronic cheques using Automated Clearinghouse (ACH) will make marginal headway there would be little chance of overtaking online credit cards. As this is an area with relatively low need for contact between banker and customer, virtual banks may be tempted to capitalize on credit card business (Shanmugam and Guru, 2003

Person-to-Person E-mail Payments: In the U.S., financial institutions are successfully launching Person-to-Person (P2P) e-mail payment systems. With these solutions, customers can make credit card payments and ACH transfers in real time to anyone with an e-mail address. It is a relatively simple process, in that, by simply adding a new front end to existing credit card and ACH payments systems to make them more convenient for consumers and businesses to transfer funds.

It is estimated that by the year 2005, Internet P2P payments in the US will grow to more than 4 billion transactions per annum.

12.7 Conclusion

Internet banking is on the rise. When viewed as another channel, its benefits are modest. However, when integrated with other channels, Internet banking becomes a powerful tool for improving customer satisfaction and increasing cross-selling opportunities. But at the same time banks must keep in mind that, every electronic channel including the Internet has its short falls which can have major consequences. Keeping track of the ever changing banking industry and the latest update in Internet technology, banks need to equip themselves for the competition. Even though there are enormous opportunities and virtual banks are on the rise 'brick and mortar' banks and transactions should not be neglected or relegated to the sidelines. This is because there are numerous aspects of banking which cannot be currently accomplished by electronic impulses.

References

BAI, "Interest in Internet Banking by Segments", JP Morgan Interviews.

Booz-Allen & Hamilton, (2003), "Processing Cost Per Transaction", JP Morgan.

Comptroller's Handbook, (1999), "Internet Banking", Comptroller of the Currency Administrator of National Banks, Oct 1999.

Forrester Research, "US EBPP Forecast."

Goldman Sachs, "Internet Penetration", Morgan Stanley Technology Research.

Harmon, S., (2001), "The Future of the Internet", Smart Investor, Issue 132, April 2001.

International Data Cooperation, "Growth in Internet Banking", epaynews.com.

Internet Banking Solutions, (2001), "Next-Generation Retail Banking", COMPAQ Inspiration Technology.

Irvine, S., (1999), "Click, Click – You're Dead", Euromoney, Sept 1999

Shanmugam, B and Guru, B.K. (2003), "Electronic Banking in Malaysia", IBBM Publications, Kuala Lumpur.

Singhal, S., (2003), "Internet Banking The Second Wave: A Banker's Guide to Internet Strategy in the Post Dotcom Era", Tata McGraw-Hill Publications.

Tower Group, (2001), "US Internet P2P Payments."

Appendix

Appendix

Major Policy Initiatives Regarding Commercial Banks since 2004

- Revised norms issued with regard to cheque Drop Box facility, delivery of cheque books over the counter and statement of accounts/pass book.
- All Scheduled Commercial Banks (SCBs) advised for sanctioning and disbursing of loans under the Prime Minister Rozgar Yojana (PMRY) for the purpose of their quarterly targets to be achieved by end-March 2005.
- Banks advised to inform their account holders, at least one month in advance of any change in the prescribed minimum balance and the charges that may be levied if the minimum balance is not maintained.
- Guidelines relating to the eligibility criteria (inclusive of minimum CRAR, non-performing asset and regulatory compliance) for declaration of dividend by commercial banks without prior approval of the RBI as well as the quantum of dividend payable (with a ceiling placed at 33.3 per cent dividend payout ratio and methods of compilation of the ratio prescribed) modified.
- Banks (excluding RRBs and LABs) advised to review at regular intervals policies and practices relating to information system (IS) audit and place the audit reports before the top management. Banks to adopt an IS Audit Policy appropriate to their level of computerisation, review the same at regular intervals in tune with industry best practices and guidelines issued by the RBI.
- Banks (excluding RRBs) advised to ensure strict compliance with the three accounting standards (No. 24, 26 and 28) relating to discounting operations, intangible assets and impairment of assets, respectively.

- All SCBs advised that the subsidy under Swarna Jayanti Shahari Rozgar Yojana (SJSRY) would be back-ended, with a lock-in period of 2 years.
- SCBs advised to strictly maintain the confidentiality of information provided by the customer for 'Know Your Customer' (KYC) compliance.
- Banks directed to scrupulously ensure that their branches do not open current accounts of entities which enjoy credit facilities (fund based or non-fund based) without specifically obtaining a no-objection certificate from the lending banks.
- The requirement of margin/security for agricultural loans up to Rs. 50,000 and in the case of agri-business and agri-clinics for loans up to Rs. 5 lakh waived.
- The exemption granted to RRBs from 'mark to market' norms in respect of the SLR securities extended for one more year, i.e. up to 2004-05.
- To give boost to infrastructure lending, banks allowed to raise long-term bonds with a minimum maturity of five years.
- The risk weight in respect of exposure by banks to public financial institutions (PFIs) raised to 100 per cent for credit risk and 2.5 per cent for market risk effective April 1, 2005.
- The extant limits on unsecured exposures by banks withdrawn, allowing banks to set their own limits for unsecured exposures. Unsecured exposures were redefined and it was clarified that Unsecured sub-standard assets would attract 20 per cent provisioning.
- The currency of the *ad hoc* Committees on Procedures and Performance Audit on Customer Services in Banks was extended by six months and they were advised to complete the work within one year from the date of their constitution and also to associate non-officials in the Committees.
- The extant guidelines on country risk management extended to cover countries where a bank has net funded exposure of one per cent or more of its assets with effect from the year ended March 31, 2005.

- Banks advised to draw a roadmap for migration to Basel II norms by the end of 2004 and prepare a quarterly review of the progress made.
- Boards of banks to oversee furnishing of requisite information of all borrowers to CIBIL and report Compliance of the same to the RBI. The role of CIBIL in dissemination of credit information was clarified. CIBIL to move towards a sufficiently diversified ownership structure with no single entity owning more than 10 per cent of its paid-up capital.
- Graded higher provisioning requirement according to the age of NPAs in 'doubtful for more than three years' category introduced for SCBs, with effect from March 31, 2005. Similar norms made applicable to RRBs on August 6, 2004.
- It was clarified that the process of identifying wilful defaulters and the mechanism related to redressal of grievances are two distinct processes. The borrower should be suitably advised before being classified as a wilful defaulter.
- Banks to fully adhere to the 'Know Your Customer' (KYC) policy adopted by their Boards: (i) for opening new accounts; (ii) for the existing accounts, where any wrong-doing is suspected or where the summation of the credit/debit transactions is more than Rs.10 lakh; and (iii) in respect of all accounts belonging to trusts, intermediaries or those operated through a mandate or power of attorney.
- The vigilance procedure in public sector banks modified. Only such vigilance cases in which an officer of the level of Scale V and above is involved are required to be referred to the Central Vigilance Commission (CVC) for advice.
- Boards of banks, under exceptional circumstances, allowed to raise single or group exposure limit by 5 per cent of capital funds.
- Banks to provide for capital charge for market risk in respect of trading book exposures (including derivatives), effective March 31, 2005. Capital charge would be introduced for securities under 'Available for Sale' (AFS) category with effect from March 31, 2006.

- Prudential norms on income recognition, asset classification and provisioning with respect to agricultural advances modified with a view to aligning the repayment dates with harvesting of crops. Effective September 30, 2004 a loan granted for short duration crops were required to be treated as NPA if the instalment of the principal or interest thereon remains unpaid for two crop seasons beyond the due date. A loan granted for long duration crops (with crop season longer than one year) is to be treated as NPA, if the instalment of principal or interest thereon remains unpaid for one crop season beyond the due date.
- All commercial banks advised to implement the measures, announced by the Union Finance Minister, for doubling the flow of credit to agriculture.
- The types of instruments to be included in the prudential limit of bank's aggregate investment in Tier-II bonds widened.
- Banks debarred from prescribing any minimum annual turnover for issuance of Gold Card since the objective of the scheme was to cover all credit worthy exporters, including the SME segment.
- Investment by banks in the mortgage backed securities (MBS) to be classified as direct lending to housing within the priority sector lending, subject to certain conditions.
- Additional measures relating to wilful defaulters introduced. These included: prohibition on additional facilities, debarment from institutional finance for floating new ventures for a period of five years, initiation of legal proceedings and foreclosure and also criminal proceedings, wherever necessary, adoption of a proactive approach for a change of management of the wilful defaulting borrower unit, incorporation of a covenant in the loan agreement barring borrowing companies to induct a person who is a director on the Board of a company which has been identified as a wilful defaulter.
- On the application of the RBI under Sub-Section (1) of Section 45 of the Banking Regulation Act, 1949, the

Government of India made an Order of Moratorium in respect of the Global Trust Bank Ltd. under Sub-Section (2) of the said Section for the period from the close of business on the July 24, 2004 and inclusive of October 23, 2004. The Government of India also issued directions to the said banking company under paragraph (2) thereof authorising payment of certain liabilities and obligations. In order to effect an amalgamation of the Global Trust Bank Ltd. with Oriental Bank of Commerce, the RBI, in exercise of the powers conferred on it by Sub-Section (4) of the said Section, prepared a scheme and forwarded it, in draft, to each of the aforesaid banking companies for suggestions and objections, if any, in terms of clause (a) of Sub-Section (6) of Section 45 *ibid* by August 7, 2004.

- Banks to insist on a declaration from the account holder for opening of current accounts, stating that he/she is not enjoying any credit facility with any other commercial bank or insist on a declaration giving particulars of credit facilities enjoyed by him/her with any other commercial bank(s). Banks also to ascertain whether he/she is a member of any other co-operative society/bank, if so, the full details thereof.
- Norms for inclusion of Self Help Groups (SHGs) for assistance under Prime Minister Rozgar Yojana (PMRY) modified.
- The monetary ceiling of the cases to be referred to the *Lok Adalats*, organised by Civil Courts, enhanced from Rs.5 lakh to Rs.20 lakh.
- Banks to convert all their equity holding into dematerialised form by the end of December 2004.
- Banks to ensure that the schedule of interest/instalment payable on advances on rural housing granted to agriculturists under 'Indira Awas Yojana and Golden Jubilee Rural Housing Finance Scheme' is linked to crop cycles.
- Banks to initiate action at their level to get the Master Policy under Personal Accident Insurance Scheme (PAIS) for KCC

holders renewed for a period of one year, on the existing terms and conditions.

- Banks to take remedial measures suggested by the Group on Frauds in the area of housing finance.
- Banks permitted to exceed the 25 per cent limit under Held to Maturity (HTM) category provided that the excess comprises only SLR securities and the total SLR securities held in the HTM category are not more than 25 per cent of their NDTLs. To enable the above, banks were allowed to shift SLR securities to the HTM category. However, no fresh non-SLR securities are permitted to be included in the HTM category once more during the year 2004-05.
- 'Yes Bank Limited' included in the Second Schedule to the Reserve Bank of India Act, 1934 with effect from August 21, 2004.
- Some recommendations of the Ganguly Working Group on Flow of Credit to SSI Sector were accepted and advised to banks for implementation. These include: (i) identification of new clusters and adoption of cluster based approach for financing the SME sector; (ii) sponsoring specific projects as well as widely publicising the successful working models of NGOs; (iii) sanctioning higher working capital limits to SSI in the North East region for maintaining higher levels of inventory; and (iv) exploring new instruments for promoting rural industry.
- Banks to open branches having no interface with customers, and which will attend exclusively to data processing, verification and processing of documents, issuance of cheque books, demand drafts etc. on requests received from other branches and other functions incidental to banking business. The licence for such branches to be issued under the 'Service Branch' category.
- The CRR applicable in respect of SCBs increased by one-half of one percentage point of their Net Demand and Time Liabilities (NDTL) in two stages - 4.75 per cent effective

September 18, 2004 and 5.0 per cent effective October 2, 2004.

- Guidelines issued for implementing the revised Model KCC Scheme of NABARD to take care of the investment credit as also working capital for agriculture and allied activities and a reasonable component for consumption needs.
- The Senior Citizens Saving Scheme (SCSS), 2004 being implemented through post offices also to be operated through all the branches of public sector banks (PSBs) which are operating 'PPF Scheme, 1968'.
- Industrial Development Bank of India (IDBI) Ltd. included in the Second Schedule to the Reserve Bank of India Act, 1934 with effect from October 11, 2004.
- Banks to implement a few more recommendations of the Vyas Committee. These included: (i) financing development of wasteland and fallow land; (ii) improving staffing in the rural areas to promote retail lending to agriculture; (iii) relying on village functionaries for credit disbursal; (iv) using individual volunteers, farmers' clubs or NGOs/SHGs as direct selling agents; (v) building synergy between good working primary agricultural credit societies and commercial banks; (vi) using Information Technology (IT) in rural branches; (vii) working out appropriate incentive structure for prompt repayment; (viii) making the rates of interest on small loans reasonable; and (ix) improving the efficiency of credit delivery to small borrowers and association with contract farming.
- Guidelines relating to the process of issue of Subordinated Debt Instruments under Tier-II and Tier-III Capital issued.
- Details of the levy of penalty on a bank to be put in the public domain in the interests of the investors and depositors. The strictures or directions on the basis of inspection reports or other adverse findings also to be placed in the public domain.
- RRBs permitted to undertake insurance business as corporate agent without risk participation subject to their fulfilling certain terms and conditions related to net worth, gross NPAs,

profitability, compliance with IRDA regulations and prudential norms and directions of the RBI.

- Banks advised to formulate a comprehensive and transparent policy covering; (i) immediate credit of local/outstation cheques; (ii) time frame for collection of local/outstation cheques; and (iii) interest payment for delayed collection.
- Banks allowed to reduce the minimum tenor of domestic/ NRO term deposits at their discretion, even below Rs.15 lakh from 15 days to 7 days.
- Banks advised to take immediate steps to ensure submission of periodical data to CIBIL and progress reports to the RBI.
- Banks advised to restructure crop loans and agricultural term loans only in respect of the overdue instalments including interest thereon as on March 31, 2004. The farmers whose loans have been restructured as above would be eligible for fresh loans. The rescheduled/restructured loans as also the fresh loans to be issued to the farmers may be treated as current due and need not be classified as NPA.
- Comprehensive guidelines on 'Know Your Customer' norms and Anti-Money Laundering Measures issued. Banks advised to frame their KYC policies incorporating the following four key elements: (i) Customer Acceptance Policy; (ii) Customer Identification Procedures; (iii) Monitoring of Transactions; and (iv) Risk Management. Similar guidelines were issued to RRBs on February 18, 2005.
- The Service Area Approach (SAA) introduced in April 1989 was reviewed and it was decided to dispense with the restrictive provisions of the scheme, while retaining the positive features such as credit planning and monitoring of the credit purveyance.
- The recommendations of the Ganguly Working Group with regard to evaluation of methods of utilisation of deposits made by foreign banks with SIDBI for shortfall in their priority sector obligation accepted. Accordingly, the amount of shortfall in priority sector obligation to be placed with

SIDBI for a tenor of three years and the funds so placed to have a graded interest rate structure.

- Banks advised to align their priority sector lendings/ investments suitably so as to comply with the extant guidelines.
- Banks advised that the due diligence in respect of members of the Nomination Committee be carried out by the Board itself.
- Comprehensive guidelines issued to banks to play a proactive role in achieving the targets set under the Swarnjayanti Gram Swarozgar Yojana (SGSY) scheme.
- Risk weight on housing loans extended by SCBs increased from 50 per cent to 75 per cent and in the case of consumer credit including personal loans and credit cards increased from 100 per cent to 125 per cent.
- Banks advised that the finance extended to employees for purchasing shares of their own companies under ESOP would continue to be treated as banks' exposure to capital market within the overall ceiling of 5 per cent, as hitherto.
- Banks maintaining currency chests advised to direct all their branches to accept coins of all denominations tendered at their counters either for exchange or for deposit in accounts.
- Banks advised to enhance the amount of consumption loan for general purposes to Rs.3,000 for people affected by *Tsunami*.
- Guidelines on receipt of foreign contributions by Associations/ Organisations in India under Foreign Contribution (Regulation) Act, 1976 for *Tsunami* Relief issued to banks.
- Banks advised to formulate suitable loan policies to finance second hand assets, both directly and through NBFCs.
- Banks advised to ensure acceptance of coins of all denominations without any restriction from the members of the public by their branches.
- Detailed prudential guidelines issued to banks on capital adequacy for implementation of the New Capital Adequacy framework under Basel II. In order to maintain consistency and harmony with international standards, banks were advised

to adopt Standardised Approach for credit risk and Basic Indicator Approach for operational risk with effect from March 31, 2007. The RBI may consider allowing some banks to migrate to Internal Rating Based (IRB) approach after developing adequate skills both in banks and at supervisory levels. Under the new framework, banks adopting Standardised Approach would use the ratings assigned only by those credit rating agencies which are identified by the RBI. Banks were also required to focus on formalizing and operationalising their internal capital adequacy assessment process (CAAP) which would serve as a useful benchmark while undertaking the parallel run with effect from April 1, 2006.

- Comprehensive guidelines issued on ownership and governance in private sector banks encompassing the minimum capital requirement, diversified ownership, procedures for acquisition and transfer of shares, 'fit and proper' criteria for the directors and important shareholders.
- Roadmap for presence of foreign banks in India laid out in two phases. In the first phase (March 2005 to March 2009) foreign banks wishing to establish presence in India for the first time could either choose to operate through branch presence or set up a 100 per cent wholly owned subsidiary (WOS), following the one-mode presence criterion. For new and existing foreign banks, it was proposed to go beyond the existing WTO commitment of 12 branches in a year. Initially entry of foreign banks would be permitted only in private sector banks that are identified by the RBI for restructuring, wherein foreign banks would be allowed to acquire a controlling stake in a phased manner. In the second phase beginning April 2009, the experience with Phase I would be reviewed and after due consultations with all stakeholders in the banking sector issues concerning extension of national treatment to WOS, dilution of stake and permitting mergers and acquisitions of any private sector banks in India by a foreign bank would be examined.

- Master circular issued to SCBs (including RRBs/LABs) in regard to matters relating to lending to the small scale industries sector.
- SCBs to report to NABARD and the RBI the progress under micro credit on a half-yearly basis as at the end of March and September of every year.
- Effective March 31, 2005, SCBs to disclose a minimum framework on their risk exposure in derivatives.
- Parameters on pilot implementation of Cheque Truncation Image Standards issued to banks.
- Draft guidelines on implementation of the New Capital Adequacy Framework issued for comments on management of operational risk.
- Banks advised to exercise caution in outsourcing of their systems and ensure that risks in this regard are minimised.
- Banks advised to implement some recommendations of the Vyas Committee. These included: (i) constitution of local advisory committee for all rural branches/group of branches; (ii) setting up of micro-finance cells at banks, central offices; and (iii) encouraging SHGs to use local book writers in association with concerned agencies promoting these SHGs for maintaining the quality of books of accounts.
- Comprehensive draft guidelines issued on securitisation of standard assets.
- The lending and deposit rates of interest restructured in the case of amounts disbursed on or Before October 31, 2003 out of RIDF IV to VII, effective April 16, 2005.
- Detailed guidelines issued to banks on rural lending under Annual Credit Plans on the basis of Potential Linked Plans (PLPs) prepared by NABARD.
- Banks to pay compensation for delayed credit under ECS/EFT/SEFT *suo moto.*
- Comprehensive draft guidelines issued on purchase / sale of non-performing assets.
- The rate of interest to be charged on group loans under SGSY linked to per capita size of the loans.

- Banks advised to put in place a Business Continuity Plan including a robust information risk management system within a fixed time frame.
- Banks advised to take necessary action to convert the existing *ad hoc* Committees on Procedures and Performance Audit of Public Services (CPPAPS) into a Standing Committee on Customer Service.
- Banks advised on the role of Customer Service Committee of the Board for monitoring the implementation of awards under the Banking Ombudsman Scheme.
- Banks permitted to shift their rural branches within the block/service area without obtaining prior approval of the RBI, subject to their complying with certain conditions.
- Banks allowed to formulate schemes for providing services at the premises of a customer within the framework of Section 23 of the Banking Regulation Act, 1949 and submit to the RBI for approval.
- Banks with capital of at least 9 per cent of the risk weighted assets for both credit risk and market risk for both HFT and AFS category of investments may treat the balance in excess of 5 per cent of securities included under HFT and AFS categories, in the IFR as Tier-I capital.
- General permission granted to banks to declare dividends, subject to the fulfilment of certain conditions, including observance of minimum CRAR and NPA ratio, subject to a ceiling of dividend Payout ratio of 40 per cent.
- Effective quarter ended June 2005, the time limit for filing the monthly and quarterly off-site returns changed to 15 days and 21 days, respectively, from the close of the relevant period for all categories of banks.
- Draft Guidelines on Corporate Debt Restructuring (CDR) proposed.
- Detailed guidelines for merger/amalgamation of private sector banks issued laying down the process of merger proposal, determination of swap ratios, disclosures, the stages at which Boards will get involved in the merger process and norms of

buying/selling of shares by the promoters before and during the process of merger.

- Comprehensive guidelines issued allowing all Regional Rural Banks (RRBs) to undertake insurance business on a referral basis, subject to certain conditions.
- The Vision Document on Payment and Settlement System 2005-08 released.
- Banks advised to initiate early action with regard to scheme for "Small Enterprises Financial Centres" (SEFCs) envisaged for forming a strategic alliance between branches of banks and SIDBI located in the clusters for improving credit flow to the SSIs sector.
- SCBs advised to put in all efforts to achieve the credit mobilisation targets under SGSY during 2005-06, including the minimum subsidy credit ratio fixed and maintain per family investment of Rs. 25,000.
- Banks allowed to extend financial assistance to Indian companies for acquisition of equity in overseas joint ventures/wholly owned subsidiaries or in other overseas companies, new or existing, as strategic investment in terms of a Board approved policy, duly incorporated in the loan policy of the bank.
- Instructions issued to banks, in supersession of all earlier instructions on settlement of claims in respect of deceased depositors, covering aspects relating to (i) access to balance in deposit account; (ii) premature termination of term deposit accounts; (iii) treatment of flows in the name of the deceased depositor; (iv) access to the safe-deposit lockers/ safe custody articles; and (v) time limit for settlement of claims.
- Banks (both in private and public sectors) need not obtain approval of the RBI for permitting any of their whole-time officers or employees (other than Chairmen/CEOs) to become Director or a part-time employee of any other company.
- Processing charges waived for all electronic products for transactions under EFT, SEFT and ECS facility involving Rs.2 crore and above with effect from June 14, 2005 up to the

period ending March 31, 2006. This was in addition to the existing waiver on transactions involving less than Rs.2 crore.

- Banks advised that while furnishing data/information to the Government or other investigating agencies they should satisfy themselves that the information is not of such a nature as will violate the provisions of the laws relating to secrecy in banking transactions.
- For the purpose of Section 20 of the Banking Regulation Act, 1949 the term "loans and advances" shall not include line of credit/ overdraft facility extended by settlement bankers to National Security Clearing Corporation Limited (NSCCL) to facilitate smooth settlement.
- The banks going for rights issues should henceforth make complete disclosure of the regulatory requirements in their offer documents.
- Banks advised to have a Board mandated policy in respect of their real estate exposure covering exposure limits, collaterals to be considered, margins to be kept, sanctioning authority/level, sector to be financed. Banks also directed to report their real estate exposure under certain heads and disclose their gross exposure to real estate sector as well as the details of the break-up in their Annual Reports.
- Banks advised to furnish information on pricing of services for products based on RTGS/SEFT/EFT/ECS infrastructure.
- Guidelines on sale/purchase of NPAs, including valuation and pricing aspects, and prudential and disclosure norms.
- Prior approval of the RBI not required for offering Internet Banking services, subject to fulfilment of certain conditions.
- The authority to grant permission to companies listed on a recognised stock exchange to hedge the price risk in respect of any commodity (except gold, silver, petroleum and petroleum products) in the international commodity exchanges/markets delegated to select commercial banks.
- The risk weight for credit risk on capital market and commercial real estate exposures increased from 100 per cent to 125 per cent.

- Guidelines issued for relief measures by banks in areas affected by unprecedented rains and floods in Maharashtra. Accordingly, banks were advised to consider granting consumption loans to the affected persons up to Rs.5,000 without any collateral and Rs.10,000 at the discretion of the branch manager, depending on the repaying capacity of the borrower.
- Banks advised to issue necessary instructions to the Controlling Offices of currency chest branches for ensuring verification of balances as per the minimum periodicity stipulated in this regard and the essential safeguards in the internal control system (such as surprise verification/joint custody, *etc.*) are adhered to.
- In view of the natural calamity and the need to provide immediate succour, banks instructed to observe minimum formalities for enabling such persons to open bank account quickly.
- Banks advised to formulate a detailed mid-term corporate plan for branch expansion for a three-year period with the approval of the Board. The plan should cover all categories of branches/offices having customer contact, including specialised branches, Extension Counters and number of ATMs *etc.* The plan should be formulated on district-wise basis giving number of branches proposed to be opened in metropolitan/urban/semi-urban/rural areas. The proposal for branch expansion with the above mentioned details should be submitted on an annual basis by December every year.
- In pursuance to the announcement made by the Union Finance Minister for stepping up credit to small and medium enterprises, public sector banks were advised to take measures to improve the flow of credit to the sector. A reporting and monitoring system for the same was also prescribed. Similar guidelines issued to private sector banks, foreign banks, RRBs and LABs on August 25, 2005.
- Banks advised to make all out efforts in achieving the targets set for increasing the credit flow to SCs/STs under priority

sector advances as well as under the Government Sponsored Schemes such as SGSY, SJSRY, SLRS and PMRY. Banks also instructed to ensure that sufficient publicity is given on the facilities extended to SCs/STs and all the instructions contained in the Master Circular on Credit facilities to SC/STs are strictly followed.

- The KYC procedure for opening accounts simplified further for those persons who intend to keep balances not exceeding rupees fifty thousand (Rs. 50,000) in all their accounts taken together and the total credit in all the accounts taken together is not expected to exceed rupees one lakh (Rs. 1,00,000) in a year. Banks may open accounts with introduction from another account holder (holding account for at least six months) who has been subjected to full KYC procedure or any other evidence as to identify and address of the customer to the satisfaction of the bank. Similar guidelines were also issued to RRBs.
- Local Area Banks were advised to submit returns and statements to the departments/offices of RBI as indicated in Annexure 'A' and 'B' enclosed to the circular issued to them on August 31, 2005.
- Banks were advised that for the purpose of Section 20 of the Banking Regulation Act, 1949, the term "Loans and advances" shall not include line of credit/overdraft facilities extended by settlement bankers to Clearing Corporation of India Ltd. (CCIL) to facilitate smooth settlement.
- Banks participating in the Pilot Cheque Truncation Project at New Delhi advised to address issues requiring urgent action including finalisation the "point of truncation" for their outward presentations and the point of processing for inward payments of the instrument, amendment of their existing internal banking and clearing manuals, use of new processing tools, deciding upon the systems for storage of inward and outward images etc.
- Guidelines on one time settlement scheme for SME accounts issued for recovery of NPAs below Rs. 10 crore.

- Banks were advised that with respect to transactions matched on the NDS-OM module, since CCIL is the central counterparty to all deals, exposure of any counterparty for a trade is only to CCIL and not to the entity with whom a deal matches. However, all government securities transactions, other than those matched on NDS-OM will continue to be physically confirmed by the back offices of the counterparties, as hitherto.
- Banks, which are nominated to import gold, were allowed to extend Gold (Metal) Loans to domestic jewellery manufacturers, who are not exporters of jewellery, subject to certain conditions.
- The policy for authorisation of the branches of banks in India liberalised and rationalised with a framework for a branch authorisation policy which would be consistent with the medium-term corporate strategy of banks and public interest. While considering applications for opening branches weightage would be given to the nature and scope of banking facilities provided by banks to common persons, particularly in underbanked areas, actual credit flow to the priority sector, pricing of products and overall efforts for promoting financial inclusion, including introduction of appropriate new products and the enhanced use of technology for delivery of banking services.
- Banks advised to implement a debt restructuring mechanism for units in the SME sector. Detailed guidelines were laid down relating to eligibility criteria for SMEs and accounts, viability criteria, prudential norms for restructured accounts, treatment of additional finance, asset classification, repeated restructuring.
- IDBI Bank Limited excluded from the Second Schedule to the Reserve Bank of India Act, 1934 with effect from April 2, 2005.
- Bank of Punjab merged with Centurion Bank with effect from October 1, 2005.

- Conversion/rescheduling of loans in the case of natural calamities, when there is delay in declaration of *Annewari* by the State Government, may be proceeded following such declaration from the District Consultative Committee (DCC) which has representatives from banks as well as the State Government and is headed by the District Collector. The limit of consumption loan to be provided to the affected persons in the state of Jammu and Kashmir and other parts of north India in the wake of the earthquake increased up to Rs.5,000 without any collateral. This limit may be enhanced to Rs.10,000 at the discretion of the branch manager, depending on the repaying capacity of the borrower. Banks may also consider provision of financial assistance for the purpose of repairs/reconstruction of dwelling units, *etc*. damaged on account of earthquake. Banks which have maintained capital of at least nine per cent of the risk weighted assets for both credit risks and market risks for both HFT and AFS categories as on March 31, 2006 would be permitted to treat the entire balance in the IFR as Tier-I capital. For this purpose, banks may transfer the entire balance in the IFR 'below the line' in the Profit and Loss Appropriation Account to Statutory Reserve, General Reserve or balance of Profit and Loss Account.
- Revised guidance note on management of operational risk issued to banks. The design of risk management framework should be oriented towards banks' own requirements dictated by the size and complexity of business, risk philosophy, market perception and the expected level of capital. The risk management systems in the bank should, however, be adaptable to changes in business, size, the market dynamics and introduction of innovative products by banks in future.
- Banks advised to provide details to the customers in their Pass Book/Account Statement regarding the credits effected through ECS. Similar approach may be adopted for capturing the sender/remittance details for other electronic payment products such as EFT, SEFT, RTGS, *etc*., as well.

- Banks advised to take appropriate action to ensure successful implementation of Swarnjayanti Gram Swarozgar Yojana (SGSY) as per the recommendations of the Central Level Coordination Committee (CLCC). The recommendations include; (i) delegation of powers to branch managers to sanction SGSY applications; (ii) ensuring disposal of all the pending applications at the end of the year in the first quarter of the succeeding year; (iii) utilising micro-finance institutions for bridging the credit gap; (iv) achieving the desired credit to subsidy ratio of 1:3; (v) furnishing of status report to Ministry of Rural Development on the under-performance of their branches; and (vi) maintaining separate record for recovery of data in respect of SGSY distinct from IRDP.
- Reverse repo rate and the repo rate under the liquidity adjustment facility (LAF) of the RBI increased by 25 basis points each with effect from October 26, 2005 to 5.25 per cent and 6.25, respectively.
- Banks advised that while considering granting advances against jewellery may keep in view the advantages of hallmarked jewellery and decide on the margin and rates of interest thereon.
- The general provisioning requirement for 'standard advances', with the exception of banks' direct advances to agricultural and SME sectors, increased from the present level of 0.5 per cent to 0.40 per cent.

Glossary of E-banking

Glossary of E-banking

Access Products: Products that allow consumers to access traditional payment instruments electronically, generally from remote locations.

Applet: A small application program that is designed to do a small, specific job.

Application: A computer program or set of programs that perform the processing of records for a specific function.

Asynchronous Transfer Mode (ATM): Method of transmitting bits of data one after another with a start bit and a stop bit to mark the beginning and end of each data unit.

Auditability: The degree to which transactions can be traced and audited through a system.

Authentication: The process of proving the claimed identity of an individual user, machine, software component or any other entity.

Authorization: The process of determining what types of activities are permitted. Usually, authorization is in the context of authentication: once you have authenticated a user, they may be authorized different types of access or activity.

Bandwidth: The transmission capacity of a computer channel or communications line

Bastion Host: A system that has been hardened to resist attack, and which is installed on a network in such a way that it is expected to potentially come under attack. Bastion hosts are often components of firewalls, or may be "outside" web servers or public access systems.

Biometrics: A method of verifying an individual's identity by analyzing a unique physical attribute.

Browser: A computer program that enables the user to retrieve information that has been made publicly available on the Internet; also permits multimedia (graphics) applications on the World Wide Web.

Byte: Fixed number of binary digits, often representing a single character.

CD-ROM: Compact Disk-Read on Memory.

Chip: An electronic device consisting of circuit elements on a single silicon chip. The most complex circuits are microprocessors, which are single chips that contain the complete arithmetic and logic units of computers.

Chip Card: Also known as an integrated circuit (IC) card. A card containing one or more computer chips or integrated circuits for identification, data storage or special-purpose processing used to validate personal identification numbers, authorize purchases, verify account balances and store personal records.

Client-Server Network: A method of allocating resources in a local area network so that computing power is distributed among computer workstations in the network but some shared resources are centralized in a file server.

Closed Network: A telecommunications network that is used for a specific purpose, such as a payment system, and to which access is restricted (also referred to as a private network).

Closed Stored Value System: A system in which value is issued and accepted by either a relatively small group of merchants, or in which the system is limited geographically (i.e., university programs and fare cards for mass transit systems).

Code: Computer programs, written in machine language (object code) or programming language (source code).

CPU: Central Processing Unit.

Cracker: A computer operator who breaks through a system's security. This can be legitimate activity, such as to test system security measures.

Cryptography: The principles, means, and methods for rendering information unintelligible and for restoring encrypted information to intelligible form (i.e., scrambling a message).

Cursor: Movable dot on the computer screen which indicates a particular position.

Cyber Mall: A set of electronic or digital storefronts linked through a common web site.

Database Administrator (DBA): The individual with authority to control the data base management system.

Dial-up: The ability of a remote user to access a system by using private or common carrier telephone lines.

Digital: Referring to communications processors, techniques, and equipment where information is encoded as a binary "1" or "0".

Digital Certification: A process to authenticate (or certify) a party's digital signature; carried out by trusted third parties.

Digital Signature: A mathematical encryption technique that associates a specific person with a given computer file and indicates that the file has not been altered since that person signed it; should not be confused with making an electronic representation of a written signature.

Distributed Transaction Processing: Application processing that involves multiple users requiring concurrent access to a single shared resource.

Domain Name: An alphanumeric name for a web site that includes both the online address and online name.

DOS: Disk Operating System.

Download: To transmit a file or program from a central computer to a smaller computer or a remote site.

Electronic Cash: The digital equivalent of dollars and cents (also referred to as digital cash).

Electronic Data Interchange (EDI): The transfer of information between organizations in machine-readable form.

Electronic Document: The digital or computer equivalent of paper documents.

Electronic Money: Monetary value measured in currency units stored in electronic form on an electronic device in the consumer's possession. This electronic value can be purchased and held on the device until reduced through purchase or transfer.

Electronic Purse: A stored value device that can be used to make purchases from more than one vendor.

E-mail: Messages people send to one another electronically from one computer to another.

Encryption (Cryptography): The process of scrambling data by a device or encoding principle (mathematical algorithms) so that the data cannot be read without the proper codes for unscrambling the data.

End-to-end Encryption: The protection of information passed in a telecommunications system by cryptographic means, from point of origin to point of destination.

Ethernet: A type of local area network originally developed by Xerox, communication takes place by means of radio frequency signals carried over coaxial cable.

File Transfer Protocol (FTP): A standard way of transferring files from one computer to another on the Internet.

Firewall: A system or combination of hardware and software solutions that enforces a boundary between two or more networks.

Flowchart: A programming tool to graphically present a procedure by using symbols to designate the logic of how a problem is solved.

Gateway: A computer that performs protocol conversion between different types of networks or applications.

GB: Giga bytes = 1 billion (million x 1,000) bytes.

Graphical User Interface (GUI): A way of communicating with a computer by manipulating icons (pictures) and windows with a mouse.

Groupware: Software that allows a group of people to work on the same data through a network, by facilitating file sharing and other forms of communication.

Hacker: A computer operator who breaks into a computer without authorization, either for malicious reasons or just to prove it can be done.

HD: Hard Disk. HD is computer's storage space. HDs are measured in mega bytes/giga bytes.

HDD: Hard Disk Drive.

Home Banking: Banking services that allow a customer to interact with a financial institution from a remote location by using a telephone, television set, terminal, personal computer, or other device to access a telecommunication system which links to the institution's computer centre.

Home Page: A screen of information made available to users through the Internet or a private intranet; it is the "main page" that users are expected to read first in order to access the other pages that comprise the web site.

Host: Also known as a host computer that is the primary or controlling computer in a computer network, generally involving data communications or a local area network.

Hypertext: Electronic documents that present information that can be connected together in many different ways, instead of sequentially.

Hypertext Mark-up Language (HTML): A set of codes that can be inserted into text files to indicate special typefaces, inserted images, and links to other hypertext documents.

Hypertext Transfer Protocol (HTTP): A standard method of publishing information as hypertext in HTML format on the Internet.

Incident Response Team: A team of computer experts (internal or external) organized to protect an organization's data, systems, and other assets from attack by hackers, viruses, or other compromise.

Indent: Space left at the beginning of a line of print.

Integrated Circuit Card (IC Card): A plastic card in which one or more integrated circuits are embedded (also called a chip card).

Internet: A worldwide network of computer networks (commonly referred to as the Information Superhighway).

Internet Service Provider (ISP): An entity that provides access to the Internet and related services, generally for a fee.

Interoperability: The compatibility of distinct applications, networks, or systems.

Intranet: A private network that uses the infrastructure and standards of the Internet and World Wide Web, but is cordoned off from the public Internet through firewall barriers.

Issuer: In a stored value or similar prepaid electronic money system, the entity which receives payment in exchange for value distributed in the system and which is obligated to pay or redeem transactions or balances presented to it.

KB: Kilo bytes = 1,000 bytes (characters).

Key: A secret value or code used in an encrypting algorithm known by one or both of the communicating parties.

LAN: Local Area Network (i.e. through the server).

Local Area Network (LAN): A network that connects several computers that are located nearby (in the same room or building), allowing them to share files and devices such as printers.

Lock and Key Protection System: A protection system that involves matching a key or password with a specific access requirement.

Logging: The storing of information about events that occurred on the firewall or network.

Magnetic Stripe: Used on debit, credit, and identification cards to store encoded information read by card readers; less secure than computer chip cards.

MB: Mega bytes = 1 million (10 lakh) bytes

Memory Card: An integrated circuit (IC) card capable of storing information only.

MHz: Mega hertz = Mega cycle = 1 million hertz or cycles per second.

Middleware: Facilitates the client/server connections over a network and allows client applications to access and update remote databases and mainframe files.

Multimedia: Audio and visual (music, pictures, graphics, animations etc.)

Navigation: Moving through a complex system of menus or help files.

Network: A group of computers connected by cables or other means and using software that enables them to share equipment and exchange information. A system of software and hardware connected in a manner to support data transmission.

Node: Any device, including servers and workstations, connected to a network. Also, the point where devices are connected.

Non-repudiable Transactions: Transactions that cannot be denied after the fact.

Off-line: Equipment or devices that are not in direct communication with the central processor of a computer system, or connected only intermittently.

On-line: Equipment or devices that communicate with a computer network. Connections can be direct (as in a LAN using dedicated connections) or indirect (as in using the Internet).

On-line Scrip: Debit accounts on the Internet or other major computer network.

On-line Service Providers (OSP): Closed network services that provide access to various computer sites or networks for a fee.

Open Network: A telecommunications network to which access is not restricted.

Open Stored Value System: A system that may be comprised of one or more electronic cash issuers of stored value that is accepted by multiple merchants or entities.

Operating System: A program that controls a computer and makes it possible for users to enter and run their own programs.

Package: A package consists of modules. The two popular modules in MS office are: (a) MS Word for word processing and (b) MS Excel for data processing.

Packet Switching: A data transmission method that routes packets along the most efficient path and allows a communication channel to be shared by multiple connections.

Password: A unique word or string of characters that a programmer, computer operator, or user must supply to satisfy security requirements before gaining access to the system or data.

Password Cracker: A software program designed to conduct an automated brute force attack on the password security controls of an information system by "guessing" user passwords.

Password Sniffer: A software program that is illicitly inserted somewhere on a network to capture user passwords as they pass through the system.

Payment System: A financial system that establishes the means for transferring money between suppliers and users of funds, usually by exchanging debits or credits between financial institutions.

Personal Identification Number (PIN): A sequence of digits used to verify the identity of a device holder.

Piggyback (Between-the-lines Entry): A means of gaining unauthorized access to a system via another user's legitimate connection.

Point of Sale (POS): A system of terminals that debits or charges a customer's account and credits or pays a merchant's account to effect payment for purchases at retail establishments.

Port: Connection for printer.

Prepaid Card: A card on which value is stored, and for which the holder has paid the issuer in advance.

Privacy: In the context of a payment system, the property that no information which might permit determination of transactions may be collected without the consent of the counterparties involved.

Protocols: A standardized set of rules that define how computers communicate with each other.

Proximity Cards: Cards that can be read from a short distance; mainly used for security and vehicle identification.

RAM: Random Access Memory (current memory as against stored memory on the Hard Disk).

Remote Payment: A payment carried out through the sending of payment orders or payment instruments.

Repudiation: The denial by one of the parties to a transaction of participation in all or part of that transaction or of the content of the communication.

Router: A computer system in a network that stores and forwards data packets between local area networks and wide area networks.

Scattering: The process of mixing the integrated circuit (IC) chip components so that they cannot be analyzed easily.

Search Engines: Software programs that are capable of locating specified information or web sites on the Internet.

Secure Electronic Transaction (SET): A set of standards jointly developed by Visa, MasterCard, and several technologies companies to facilitate secure credit card transactions over the Internet.

Secure Socket Layer (SSL): A protocol for providing data security during transmission using data encryption, server authentication, and message integrity.

Server: A computer that provides services to another computer (the client).

Settlement: An act that discharges obligations with respect to funds or securities transfers between two or more parties.

Settlement System: A system used to facilitate the settlement of transfers of funds.

Simple Mail Transfer Protocol (SMTP): A protocol used to transfer electronic mail between computers on the Internet.

Smart Card: A card with a computer chip embedded, on which financial, health, educational, and security information can be stored and processed.

Specification: Documents that contain basic detailed data.

Spoofing: An attempt to gain access to a system by posing as an authorized user.

Standards: The rules under which analysts, programmers, operators, and other personnel in an information service organization work.

Stored Value Card: A card that stores prepaid value via magnetic stripe or computer chip.

Structured Query Language (SQL): A query language used to manipulate large databases.

SVGA: Special Video Graphics Adapter (for quick display of graphics).

System Integrity: The quality that a system has when it performs its intended function in an unimpaired manner, free from deliberate or inadvertent manipulation of the system.

System Specification: A baseline specification containing all the essential computer-based business system documentation. It is completed at the end of the Development Phase.

Systemic Risk: The risk that the failure of one participant in a funds transfer system, or in financial markets generally, to meet its required obligations will cause other participants or financial institutions to be unable to meet their obligations when due.

Systems Analysis: The performance, management, and documentation of the four phases of the life cycle of a business system: study, design, development, and operation.

Tamper-evident: The capacity of devices to show evidence of physical attack.

Tamper-proof: The proven capacity of devices to resist all attacks.

Tamper-resistant: The capacity of devices to resist physical attack up to a certain point.

Telecommunications: Data transmission between a computing system and remotely located devices via telephone lines, cable, or wireless technology.

Telnet: A protocol that permits users to access a remote terminal or another computer through a network; widely used on the Internet.

Threat Monitoring: The analysis, assessment, and review of audit trails and other data collected for the purpose of searching out system events that may constitute violations or attempted violations of system security.

Throughput: The total amount of useful work performed by a data processing system during a given period of time.

Topology: The arrangement of nodes usually forming a star, ring, tree, or bus pattern.

Traceability: The degree to which transactions can be traced to the originator or recipient (also referred to as auditability).

Transferability: In electronic money systems, the degree to which an electronic balance can be transferred between devices without interaction with a central authority.

Transmission Control Protocol/Internet Protocol (TCP/IP): A standard format for transmitting data in packets from one computer to another, on the Internet and within other networks. TCP deals with the construction of the data packets while IP routes them from machine to machine.

Trap Door: A concealed and unauthorized entrance into a computer operating system, designed by the programmer.

Trojan Horse: A program that appears to perform a useful function and sometimes does so quite well but also includes an unadvertised feature, which is usually malicious in nature.

Truncation: Dropping off part of a character string either to conserve space or because of limited space.

Trusted Computer System: A system that employs sufficient assurance measures to allow its use for simultaneous processing of a range of sensitive or classified information.

Trusted Third Party: A reputable entity that authenticates one or more parties to an electronic transaction. The authentication process generally involves the issuance and administration of digital certificates.

Uniform Resource Locator or Universal Resource Locator (URL): A way of specifying the location of available information on the Internet.

Upload: To transmit a file to a central computer from a smaller computer or a remote location.

Usenet: A set of many newsgroups distributed via the Internet.

VDU: Visual Display Unit.

Virtual Corporations: Corporations that have no official physical site presence and are made up of diverse geographically dispersed or mobile employees.

Virus: A program with the ability to reproduce by modifying other programs to include a copy of itself. It may contain destructive code that can move into multiple programs, data files, or devices on a system and spread through multiple systems in a network.

Vulnerability: A weakness in system security procedures, system design, implementation, internal controls, etc., that could be exploited to violate system security.

Web Page: A screen of information supporting the home page of a web site.

Web Site: The collection of an entity's home page and other proprietary pages located on the World Wide Web.

Wide Area Network (WAN): A communications network that covers a wide geographic area, such as state or country, using high speed long distance lines or satellites provided by a common carrier.

World Wide Web (web, www): A sub network of the Internet through which information is exchanged via text, graphics, audio, and video.

Worm: A program that scans a system or an entire network for available, unused space in which to run. Worms tend to tie up all computing resources in a system or on a network and effectively shut it down.

Bibliography

Bibliography

Agarwal N, Agarwal R, Sharma P, "Ebanking for Comprehensive E-democracy: An Indian Discernment" www.JIBC.com/e-banking, 2000

Age of Universal Banking. African Business, June 2001 Issue.

Are German-type Universal Banks Superior in Performance to other Types of Universal Banks? By: Wonsik Sul; Joon Seok Oh. Journal of Financial Management & Analysis, Jul-Dec. 99, Vol. 12 Issue 2.

Arora, Kalpana, 'Indian Banking: Managing Transformation through IT', IBA Bulletin, Vol. XXV, No. 3, March 2003.

ATM Transactions Pip Credit Cards, *Economic Times*, May 31, 2003.

Avasthi, G.P.M., 'Information Technology in Banking: Challenges for Regulators', Prajnan, Vol. XXIX, No. 4, 2000.

Bajaj, K.K., 'E-Commerce Issues in the Emerging Hi -Tech. Banking Environment', The Journal of The Indian Institute of Bankers, Jan-March 2000.

Bakshi, S., 'Corporate Governance in Transformation Times', IBA Bulletin, 2003.

Balasubramanya, S., IT Wave Breaks over Banking, *The City*, Aug.-Sept. 2002

Bank Quest (various issues).

Banu, Hasan, Outsourcing Marketing; A New Mantra in Banking Industry, *Southern Economist*, Sept. 1, 2004.

Bhasin, T.M., 'E-Commerce in Indian Banking', IBA Bulletin, Vol. XXIII, Nos. 4 & 5, (April–May 2001.

Bimil Jalan, "Strengthening Indian Banking and Finance - Progress and Prospects", The Bank Economist Conference, India, 2002.

Biswas, S, 'Information Technology in Service Sector- A Vision for India', available at www.tifac.org.in

Booz-Allen & Hamilton, "Processing Cost Per Transaction", JP Morgan, 2003.

Booz-Allen & Hamilton, Inc., "Booz-Allen's Worldwide Survey Revealed A Huge Perception Gap Between Japanese and American/European Banks Regarding Internet Banking.", 1997

Booz-Allen & Hamitton, Processing Cost Per Transaction, JP Morgans,2003

BPOs to Provide Jobs in New Areas, *The Tribune*, June 21, 2006.

Changy, "Dynamics of Banking Technology Adoption: An Application to Internet Banking" Department of Economics, University of Warwick, January 2003.

Chhabra, Sangeeta, Business Process Outsourcing–Finance & Accounting: An Introduction, *The Management Accountant*, Vol. 41, No.8, 2006.

Comptroller's Handbook, "Internet Banking", Comptroller of the Currency Administrator of National Banks, October 1999.

Comptroller's Handbook, Internet Banking, *Comptroller of the Currency Administrator of National Banks*, October 1999.

Conflict of Interest in Universal Banking: Bank Lending, Stock Underwriting, and Fund Management. By Ber, Hedva; Yafeh, Yishay; Yosha, Oved. Journal of Monetary Economics, Feb. 2001, Vol. 47 Issue 1.

Consolidation and Universal Banking. By Saunders, Anthony. *Journal of Banking* & Finance, Feb. 99, Vol. 23 Issue 2-4.

Corrocher, N., "Does Internet banking substitute traditional banking? Empirical Evidence from Italy," Working Paper, CESPRI, No. 134, November 2002.

Diniz, E, "Web Banking In USA," Journal of Internet Banking and Commerce, Vol.3, No. 2, June 1998.

Egland, Kori L., Karen Furst, Daniel E. Nolle, Douglas Robertson, "E-banking over the Internet", Quarterly Journal, Vol. 17, No. 4, Office of Comptroller of the Currency, December 1998.

EPW Research Foundation, Increasing Concentration of Banking Operations, *Economic & Political Weekly*, Vol. XLI, No.11, 2006.

Expansion of Commercial Banking Powers ... or, Universal Banking is the Cart, not the Horse. By: Boyd, John H. Journal of *Banking* & Finance, Feb99, Vol. 23 Issue 2-4.

Experts Split on Safety of Universal Banks. By: Seiberg, Jaret. American Banker, 11/14/97, Vol. 162 Issue 220.

Furst, K; Lang, W., William and Nolle, E., Daniel, "Internet Banking: Developments and Prospects," Working Paper, Center for Information Policy Research, Harvard University, April 2002.

Ganesh, S., 'Frauds in A Computerized Environment', IBA Bulletin, Vol. XXIII, 2001.

Garg, I.K., 'Indian Banking in Transition: Some Management Challenges', IBA Bulletin, Vol. XXV, No. 3, March 2003.

Gupta, Ankur, Data Protection in Consumer E-banking, *Journal of Internet Banking and Commerce*, Vol.11, No.1, 2006.

Gupta, R P., 'Banking in the New Millennium: Strategic Management Issues', IBA Bulletin, Vol. XXIII, No. 3, March 2001.

Gupta, S.C., Banking Industry Vision 2010, *IBA Committee Report*, November 2003.

Harman, S, The future of the Internet Banking, *Smart Investor*, Issue 132, April 2001.

Harmon, S., "The Future of the Internet", Smart Investor, Issue 132, April 2001.

Hasan, I., "Do Internet Activities Add Value? The Italian Bank Experience", Working Paper, Federal Reserve Bank of Atlanta, New York University, 2002.

Information Technology (various issues).

International Data Cooperation, 'Growth in Internet Banking', available at www.epaynews.com

Internet Banking Solutions, "Next-Generation Retail Banking", COMPAQ Inspiration Technology, 2001.

Irvine, S., "Click, Click – You're Dead", Euromoney, September 1999.

Jalan, B., 'Strengthening Indian Banking and Finance: Progress and Prospectus', IBA Bulletin, Vol. XXV, No. 3, March 2003.

Janice, David and Dennis, "Click and Mortar of Retail Banking A Case Study in Hong Kong," Nanyang Business School, Nanyang Technological University, 2002.

K Arvind, Surjit, 'Internet Banking: Concepts, Risks and Issues', available at www.rbi.org.in

Laxman, G. (2005), ATM Services and Perceptions of Users; A Case Study of Andhra Bank, *Southern Economist*, Vol. 44, No.5, 2005.

Leeladhar, V. 'Contemporary and Future Issues in Indian Banking', Available at www.rbi.org.

Maheshwari, S.N. *Banking Law and Practi*ce, Kalyani Publishers.

Malhotra, Pooja and Singh Balwinder, New Revolution in the Indian Banking Industry; Internet Banking, *Punjab Journal of Business Studies*, Vol.1, No.1, 2005.

Malhotra, Pooja and Singh, Balwinder, New Revolution in the Indian Banking Industry, *Punjab Journal of Business Studies*, April-Sept., Vol.1, No.1, 2005.

Marwaha, Rajesh, Infotrends in Indian Banking Industry, *Punjab Journal of Business Studies*, Vol. 1, No.1, 2005.

Mishra A. K. 'Internet Banking in India' available at www.banknetindia.com

Mohan, R., 'Transforming Indian Banking: In Search of a Better Tomorrow', IBA Bulletin, Vol. XXV, No. 3, March 2003.

Nair, S.N., 'E-Commerce and The Emergence of E-banking', IBA Bulletin, Vol. XXII, No. 10, (October), No. 12, December 2000.

Narayana V., Nuts and Bolts of Internet Banking, *Investment World*, July 16, 2000.

Nayyar, *Taxmann's Banking Law Practice in India*, Taxmann Publishers.

Official web site of Ministry of Information Technology, Government of India. http://www.mit.gov.in/eg/home.asp, 2003

Patrick R Anil, The Tech Factor in Banking Technology in Banking, *Network Magazine*, May 2003.

Patrick R Anil, The Tech Factor in Banking-Technology in Banking, *Network Magazine*, May 2003.

Perumel, Vignesen & Shanmugam, Bala, 'Internet Banking: Boon or Bane?' Available at www.arreydev.com

Prasad, P.S.R., Cost Benefit Analysis (Automated Teller Machine), *The Management Accountant,* Vol.6, No.8, 2006.

Rahul Sachitanand, ATM Will Deliver Much More, *The Economic Times*, Feb. 13, 2003

Ramanathan, A., Financial Liberalization and Economic Development – The Theory and Experience, *IEJ,* Vol. 46, No.1, 1998.

Rangarajan, S.C., Financial Sector Reforms: Managing Changes, *PNB, M.R.*, Vol. 18, No. 11, 2000.

Rangarajan, S.C., Financial Sector Reforms: The Indian Experience, *RBI Bulletin*, July 2000.

Reserve Bank of India, Report on Currency and Finance (various issues).

Sandhu, H.S. & Soch, 'Impact of Information Technology on the Indian Banking Sector', Edited Book, Economic Reforms in India – From First to Second Generation and Beyond, Deep & Deep Publications, New Delhi, 2003.

Shanmugam, B and Guru, B.K., "Electronic Banking in Malaysia", IBBM Publications, Kuala Lumpur, 2003.

Shapiro, C, 'Will E-Comm. Erode Liberty', Harvard Business Review, May-June 2000.

Shastri, R.V, 'Technology for Banks in India- Challenges', IBA Bulletin, Vol. XXIII, No. 3, March 2001.

Singhal, S, Internet Banking-The second wave, *Banker's guide to Internet Strategy in the Post Dotcom Era*, Tata McGraw-Hill Publications, 2003.

Singhal, S., "Internet Banking The Second Wave: A Banker's Guide to Internet Strategy in the Post Dotcom Era", Tata McGraw-Hill Publications, 2003.

The European Influence. By: Stein, Robert W. Best's Review, October 2000, Vol. 101 Issue 6.

The Future of Universal Banking. By: Rich, Georg; Walter, Christian. CATO Journal, Fall 93, Vol. 13 Issue 2.

Trivedi, A. K., 'Indian Banking: Managing Transformation', IBA Bulletin, Vol. XXV, No. 3, (March) Vol. XXV, No. 3, March 2003.

Universal Banking and US Banking in the 1990s. By: Cameron, Colleen W.. International Journal of Social Economics, 1995, Vol. 22 Issue 4.

Universal Banking By: Benston, George J. Journal of Economic Perspectives, Summer 94, Vol. 8 Issue 3.

Universal Banking is Government's Aim. Emerging European Markets, October 97, Vol. 1 Issue 2.

Universal Banking: A Shareholder Value Perspective. By: Walter, Ingo. European Management Journal, Aug. 97, Vol. 15 Issue.

Unnithan, C.R. and Swatman, P., E-banking Adaptation and Dot.com Viability-A Comparison of Australian and Indian Experiences in the Banking Sector, Working Paper, School of management Information Systems, Deakin University, No.14, 2001

Unnithan, C.R. and Swatman, P., E-banking Adaptations and Dot.Com violability - A Comparison of Australian and Indian Experience in Banking Sector, Working Paper, School of Management & Information System, Deakin University, No.14, 2001.

Varshney, P. N., *Banking Law and Practice*, Kalyani Publishers.

Index

Index

W